Rays of Research on
Real Estate Development

Rays of Research on Real Estate Development

Jaime Luque

BEP BUSINESS EXPERT PRESS

First published in 2017 by
Business Expert Press, LLC
222 East 46th Street, New York, NY 10017
www.businessexpertpress.com

ISBN-13: 978-1-63157-600-3 (print)
ISBN-13: 978-1-63157-601-0 (e-book)

Business Expert Press Finance and Financial Management Collection

Collection ISSN: 2331-0049 (print)
Collection ISSN: 2331-0057 (electronic)

Cover and interior design by S4Carlisle Publishing Services
Private Ltd., Chennai, India

First edition: 2017

10 9 8 7 6 5 4 3 2 1

Printed in the United States of America.

Dedication

This book would not have been possible without the numerous contributions of students who took my "Regional and urban economics" course at the University of Wisconsin, Madison. I dedicate this book to them.

Abstract

Real estate development accounts for one of the major economic sectors in most countries, yet during the last two decades research on this important topic has been scattered. This textbook brings together some of the most important results on this subject. The book is written in a pedagogical way and covers crucial aspects of this industry such as growth management and real options, land use regulations, mixed housing developments, taxes, externalities, housing affordability problems, land prices and uncertainty, public infrastructures, and housing supply.

This textbook is an excellent source for an advance course in real estate development that attempts to cover important contributions in this area. The book is accompanied with multiple choice questions to test students' assimilation of the material.

Keywords

externalities, growth management and real options, housing supply, land use regulations, housing affordability problems, land prices and uncertainty, mixed housing developments, public infrastructures, real estate development, taxes

Contents

Preface

In collaboration with Eduardo De La Torre

The process of real estate development in an urban landscape is multi-faceted and multidisciplinary in nature for a variety of reasons. Although there is often the misconception that real estate development is an endeavor pursued and managed purely by the private interests of firms and actors, this couldn't be further from the truth. If this were the case, profit-maximizing principles would dictate the development and layouts of our cities, natural resources would be exploited whenever net economic benefit could be extracted, urban landscapes would not take into account the welfare of its populace, and vulnerable communities would be subject to the predatory nature of the free market.

Although real estate development does respond to market forces of supply and demand, it is subject to certain restrictions imposed by government actors who act in the interest of creating sustainable cities that both encourage productivity, mobility, and economic growth, but that also consider the benefits of creating communities that are walkable, enjoyable, and safe. The goal is to create a prudent development strategy that encompasses interests that benefit the private and public sectors.

An important aspect of this strategy is compact development that repurposes land within existing infrastructure. This means redeveloping existing land with a current use that no longer meets the goals of both private and public actors with the goal of creating net benefit for both. This concept is beneficial to real estate developers and investors that represent private interests because this reduces the costs for land and infrastructure development. Instead of creating a project beyond the limits of the city, and having to start from scratch in terms of infrastructure, it is cheaper to develop within the city and revitalize land and structures. This concept is also beneficial to the private interests of businesses because the increased economic activity that ensues attracts additional investment and spending power. It is also in the best interest of public interests such as local governments because it reduces their costs of providing public services such as fire and police protection, utilities such as electricity, sewage, and water, as well as a variety of other public amenities.

Another goal of this strategy is creating cities that encourage walkability. Real estate developers and investors benefit from this strategy because it increases sales. Creating more walkable access to storefronts encourages more spending, which naturally increases sales prices. This increased economic activity naturally benefits the individual business owners as well. It is also in the interest of local governments to adopt policy encouraging walkable spaces because property and sales tax revenue increases, which allows these governments to more effectively provide resources to its constituents.

The last example of smart development strategy encompasses the creation of a diverse range of choices and land uses, building types, transportation models, housing types, and commercial spaces. This diverse land use is beneficial to developers and investors because it results in increased sales and investment values within real assets. It benefits businesses because increased mix-use amenities allow them to attract employees as well as customers. Finally, it creates an opportunity for local governments to increase their tax base from higher property taxes and new residents.

Public policy is an essential tool that government actors use to manage development in a way that allows them to meet certain goals within their jurisdictions. Policy is used to shape the regulatory landscape in which real estate developers conduct their business. Policy can shape the kind of development that goes in within an area, what certain land uses are permitted within a specific location, and which land isn't available for further development. These kinds of regulations help government entities determine the layout and use of city spaces, which, at an aggregate, determine their long-term goals. Different cities have different goals when it comes to public policy. This book explores several aspects of the real estate development process, and how different actors interact within a common framework to create sustainable cities.

We begin our analysis by exploring the relationship between market volatility and irreversible investment in real estate development. This helps us understand the real estate development process from the framework of an investor, which allows us to gain some insight into key decision-making processes. We extend this analysis to explore the concept and tools used in growth management, namely, we explore the different results that followed the implementation of urban growth boundaries within certain cities. This provides important knowledge to urban planners and policy makers in pursuing their development goals moving forward. Through using tools such as Urban Growth Boundaries, cities can concentrate housing development in the areas that they desire, while also removing the allure for landowners outside the boundary to brush off other forms of development in hopes that their parcels may one day attract high-paying residential and multifamily developers.

We also perform a cost–benefit analysis of land use regulation, which we use to construct an overall view of what land regulation entails, as well as setting a framework for the cost–benefit analysis of other public policy options. We introduce concepts such as negative and positive externalities which are key concepts in understanding policy goals. We use the cost–benefit framework to extend our analysis to the costs of habitat conservation. We seek to analyze how preexisting development restrictions affect the cost of habitat protection. As previously mentioned, conserving certain environmental and natural resources is extremely important when creating sustainable cities.

We further our study of the real estate development process by introducing a budgetary framework for housing development. An example of public policy aimed at creating affordable housing are housing assistance programs, which are employed to stimulate new construction or restoration of subsidized price housing for lower-income households. We use this analysis to understand methods of creating affordable cities that serve the interests of the disadvantaged. We also explore the role that public policy has on racial patterns within cities. Eliminating segregation within cities is a goal that public policy seeks to find an answer to. We analyze minority access to new housing developments, as well as the impact on their access to filtered units in moving chains initiated by new housing starts. This can give us some insight on steps we can take to ensure communities create environments where social mobility is possible, and where people aren't put at a disadvantage based on racial background.

It is evident that the real estate development market plays a huge role in the creation of jobs within a city. This book explores the role that real estate development has on the growth of employment within a city. We also seek to uncover the effects of housing prices on labor migration and analyze how traditional neighborhood development has changed over the years, primarily focusing on the creation of pedestrian and transit-friendly environments, as well as well as the establishment of mixed land uses. These aspects will help the reader learn how vibrant cities attempt to incorporate this into their policy goals for better communities.

We move on to discuss how fiscal policy affects the development process. We explore topics such as impact fees and property taxes, which are used to create incentives for developers. We analyze the role that different taxation methods play in real estate development and the supply and demand side behavior of both developers and consumers. We use this as a foundation to explore the trends in construction, also referred to the construction cycle. We seek to uncover the dynamics of housing supply in urban environments, with the aim of understanding how to create a sustainable level of housing stock that meets certain policy goals.

We finish our analysis by discussing several topics such as environmental contamination risk, the uncertainty of the land price market, the role of affordable housing measures in low-income communities, as well as the development of public infrastructure with the aim of spurring economic growth. We seek to use all the tools presented to create a framework from which to analyze real estate development and make sustainable policy decisions that enable us to meet the dynamic goals of different urban environments.

PART I

Growth Management and Real Options

CHAPTER 1

Volatility, Competition, and Investments

In collaboration with Alexandra Piechowicz and Nicholas Sanders

The possibility of failure deters many individuals from investing time or money into something, in particular when the probability of an attractive return is low or the projected revenue is truly uncertain. For example, a rational individual would not pay $50,000 for a lottery ticket if his or her chances of winning $75,000 were one-in-a-million. Risking $50,000 is likely not worthwhile when the potential return on his or her investment is only 50 percent and the likelihood of losing the investment is almost inescapable. Here, the expected benefit (multiplying the probability of success by the $75,000) is $37,500, whereas the cost for the lottery ticket is $50,000. In essence, purchasing the lottery ticket poses a risk far greater than the expected return. While the aforementioned example is an extreme and unlikely circumstance, rational thinking and analytical deliberation are essential to the many realms of large capital investment where uncertainty is inevitable.

Bulan, Mayer, and Somerville (2009) explore the relationship between market volatility and irreversible investment in real estate development in Vancouver, Canada, examining how idiosyncratic and systematic risk and competition affect firms' decisions to undertake certain projects. The goal of the authors is to demonstrate the existence of a negative relationship between idiosyncratic risk and irreversible asset investment with a focus on the real options model. In addition, the authors prove a negative relationship between market volatility and real estate investment consistent with capital asset pricing model (CAPM). Bulan, Mayer, and Somerville (2009) attempt to show that competition within development reduces the impact of return volatility on investment. They seek to establish that competition is a driver for investment and that delays in investment tend to occur during a market downturn in which competition is reduced. The authors analyze data collected between 1979 and 1998 and compare their results to existing literature specific to competition and the real options framework.

The data that the authors analyze was collected from 1,214 strata projects built between January 1979 and February 1998 in Vancouver, Canada. This nearly twenty-year period exhibited four boom-and-bust cycles (1982, 1986, 1991, and 1996) during which the growth of strata projects consistently surpassed the growth of single-family developments. The authors provide information about the number of projects in a given calendar year and the average size of the projects for that year in units per project. Using the sale prices of all strata transactions between 1979 and 1998—obtained from the British Columbia Assessment Authority (BCAA)—the authors compile a repeat sales index for each of the seven sections of the city—three unique and four consolidations on the basis of similarities. Using a combination of autoregressive models and GARCH models, the authors compute expected price appreciation, project-specific discount rates, systematic risk, return volatility, and the magnitude of competition.

The author's primary model for analysis is the real options model. The theory supporting the model is that firms should apply a higher user cost to new investments in real estate when returns are volatile, reflecting the option to delay that is lost when investment occurs. The authors believe that this model is valid because the traditional CAPM model already predicts lower investments in volatile markets. Higher volatility is linked to greater nondiversifiable risk and thus a higher required rate of return from investors. Thus, the authors find clear support for the negative relationship between investment and idiosyncratic risk in existing models and intuition. The second component of the real options model is the effect of competition on investment. Local competition posed by proximate potential developments can erode the value of the option to delay irreversible investment and make firms more likely to develop by lowering the cost of forfeiting their option.

The authors first find that coefficients for neighborhood price-level indexes and volatilities, building type, project size variables, and neighborhood fixed effects generally conform to the real options model. Price coefficients are expectedly greater than one, indicating that the developers choose to develop a parcel more quickly when neighborhood prices are higher. The coefficient on the volatility of condo returns is less than one suggesting that developers wait longer when volatility is higher, even when controlled for price levels. One standard deviation increase in condo return volatility decreases the monthly hazard rate, reflecting the probability of development as a function of time alone, by 13 percent which leads to a 9-percent decrease in prices. The authors then controlled for market risk by multiplying the neighborhood condo risk rate by the volatility of the TSE 300 Index. Here, one standard deviation increase in the average market volatility across neighborhoods leads to an 8-percent decline in the hazard rate, whereas an equivalent standard deviation increase in idiosyncratic volatility leads to an 11-percent decrease in the hazard rate.

One additionally significant variable is the risk-free interest rate. One percentage point increase in the risk-free rate leads to a 52-percent decline in the monthly hazard rate. However, the drift rate, which measures expected capital appreciation, was found to be insignificant and independent of the hurdle rate, which conforms to the real options model.

Further results show how volatility correlates with pricing and development through examining expected price appreciation. The statistically significant coefficient on expected price appreciation is above one while the coefficient on negative expected price appreciation is less than one. This demonstrates that holding price constant, development is more likely when prices are rising faster *and* when prices are falling faster since the negative coefficient produces a positive effect on the hazard rate when combined with negative price changes. The authors attribute this contradiction to the fact that rising prices can help developers overcome liquidity constraints and pursue a larger number of projects leading to a higher hazard rate. Conversely, developers race each other to build when prices are quickly falling due to an iteration of the prisoner's dilemma in which both developers choose to build rather than being beaten to the market, which causes a cascade of development and falling prices.

The authors next address the second component of their hypothesis regarding the relationship between competition and the hazard rate. Their results show that volatility has a smaller impact on option exercise in areas that face greater potential competition. As more competitors surround a project, its hazard rate of construction becomes less sensitive to volatility. Given the mean number, 23, of potential projects, measured as the number of potential projects within 4 years and 1 kilometer, 1 standard deviation increase in return volatility leads to a 13-percent decline in new construction. However, if the number of competitors increases by 50 percent, the equivalent standard deviation increase in volatility leads to only a 9-percent decline. The authors additionally found that competition was not significantly related to any other variable than volatility and the coefficient on competition in isolation was insignificant.

The authors conclude that builders delay development during periods of greater exposure to idiosyncratic and market risk. They also conclude that competition in the local market significantly reduces the effect of option exercise in respect to volatility. Given these two conclusions, the authors find sufficient support for the real options model because the interaction between volatility and competition does not appear to affect the user cost of a reversible investment. The authors expand their discussion to address the common conception that developers irrationally overbuild. However, the authors' results show that rational and strategic decision-making processes cause developers to start more projects as prices fall. A more salient conclusion discussed is that the real options model has major implications for how developers time their investment. If competition decreases in recession, the real options model implies that developers now find more value in delaying their irreversible investment. Conversely, boom times leads to higher competition, which decreases the value of the option and delaying investment. The relationship between volatility, competition, and investment timing leads to a broader conclusion that understanding the real options model can help explain the cyclical component of real estate investment across the economy.

Bulan, Mayer, and Somerville (2009) rely heavily on the real options model to support the arguments in their paper. Another scholar, Francesco Baldi—who acknowledges real options as imperative to real estate development and investment—proposes a new methodology that *quantifies* the values of said options based on a portfolio view to complement the real options model (see Baldi 2013). Baldi identifies real options as a combination of timing—immediate and deferrable—and scaling—up and down—strategies. This flexibility is extremely important to real estate development as unforeseen circumstances may derail the progress of an investment; real options help developers adjust to these new conditions so that they can maximize and retain projected profits. The valuation framework that Baldi proposes consists of "binomial trees"—bottom, intermediate, and upper—that represent the three stages of development, respectively, preconstruction, completion of the first stage, and the final completion of the project. The value—based on expected land appraisal—of a real option varies depending on when—during which of the aforementioned stages—the decision is made. Flexibility and the availability of real options are especially favorable to developers as market volatility increases; changes to the itinerary may be crucial for profit maximization. All in all, real options are best taken into consideration through a thorough portfolio approach when appraising a development. An extensive analysis of market conditions, development progress, and expected property values can ensure that investors will receive a desirable payoff.

Bulan, Mayer, and Somervile (2009) identify several weaknesses in their analysis. The first arises from strata data, which is filed when a building is very close to completion. Therefore, there is no reliable start date for construction which is relevant when evaluating option exercise, or when the choice whether or not to invest occurs. To compensate, the authors added a lag time of 1 year to the date indicated on the strata plan. This lag time is an estimation based on an observation that 59 percent of new multifamily projects are completed within 1 year from the construction start date. A second weakness is found within the project-specific discount rate. The model used to find the rate makes the assumption that real estate market is in perpetual equilibrium. The authors believe that this model is inconsistent with the market history marked by periods of disequilibrium. Instead of using the project-specific discount rate, a substitute is implemented from the CAPM model in which the project-specific rate is estimated by simply adding a market risk premium to the risk-free rate. A third weakness is the existence of dual options inherent in the sequential nature of real estate development. Developers can invest and disinvest by repurposing or terminating projects before final completion. Since strata plans are filed very close to completion, projects that were terminated or repurposed will not be included in strata data and excluded from analysis. To compensate for this weakness, the authors artificially censor the data by truncating the sample from 1994 when there was a downturn in development.

The authors offer the solid foundation of a reliable model to apply to real estate development in macroeconomic analysis. It offers a convincing perspective on the cyclical nature of the market and can help explain how developers time their investments. Given this basis, researchers could apply this model to other markets other than Vancouver to establish generalizability and determine how results differ across markets using the real options model. The research, here, was conducted prior to the subprime crisis, so it would be relevant to examine whether the unprecedented downturn has affected developer's investment behavior and if the real option model has different implications in today's altered environment.[1] A longitudinal study using the real options model across a diverse sample of markets across the United States would likely provide useful insights into today's resurging market and the reasons for development given current risk and competitive landscapes.

Multiple Choice Questions

1. Many scholars argue that market power is essential to attaining greater revenue when volatility is increased, even positing that one firm's strategic advantage may discourage other firms from developing. However, Bulan, Mayer, and Somervile (2009) use the results of external research to explain that competition *is* favorable to a market in which uncertainty is high. Which of the following is true regarding competition in real estate development?

    a. Real estate is a perfectly competitive, homogenous market in which locations are perfect substitutes for each other

---

[1]See Mian and Sufi (2014) for an economic analysis of the recent subprime mortgage crisis and its consequences.

b. Holding price constant, development stagnates when prices *rise* quickly in a competitive market

c. Holding price constant, development stagnates when prices *fall* quickly in a competitive market

d. **None of the above**

Explanation: The correct answer is (d): none of the above statements are correct. (a) is incorrect because although homogeneity is necessary for "perfect competition," real estate—in the case of development—is *not* homogenous. According to the Novy-Marx (2005) research included in the paper, opportunity costs differ between potential sites due to varying preexisting uses and withstanding structures. The locations are so unique that they cannot be considered perfect substitutes. (b) and (c) are also incorrect because development is actually *more likely* to occur when prices change rapidly, both negatively and positively. This situation is called a "panic equilibrium" in which competition is increased due to the changes in price. During a "panic equilibrium," new developments will proliferate before prices change too drastically to avoid losing a location or missing an opportunity.

2. During the two-decade period of focus, there were four main booms of strata development in Vancouver. According to Bulan, Mayer, and Somervile (2009), which of the following statements can be used to explain the massive growth of condominium construction in 1982, 1986, 1991, and 1996?

a. The booms were triggered by an abundance of undeveloped land in the Vancouver metropolitan area

b. **Chinese immigration during the late 1980s triggered an increase in property prices as demand for housing skyrocketed**

c. The "cosmopolitan" trend of condominium ownership over single-family homes continued to grow since the early 1970s

d. All of the above

Explanation: The correct answer is (b): Chinese immigration during the late 1980s triggered an increase in property prices as demand for housing increased. Between 1988 and 1990, real estate prices soared as a wave of immigrants from Hong Kong moved to Vancouver following instability in China and the Tiananmen Square protests of 1989. (a) is incorrect because the growth of condominium developments surpassed the growth of single-family developments due to the *scarcity* of undeveloped land. High-rise, multifamily strata projects were able to house more people while taking up significantly less space than single-family homes. (c) is incorrect because according to local Vancouver speculators, the general acceptance and trend of condominium ownership was not exhibited until the mid-1980s.

3. The British Columbia Assessment Authority (BCAA) provided Bulan, Mayer, and Somervile (2009) with the majority of the data that was used in their study. Which of the following information concerning real estate development in Vancouver between 1979 and 1998 was not obtained—both directly and/or through analysis—by the authors of this paper?

   a. **The start date of construction**
   b. The expected price appreciation
   c. The number of units per project
   d. Prices of all condominium transactions

Explanation: The correct answer is (a): the Start date of construction. (a) is correct because developers typically file a strata plan—converting a single title for the parcel of land into multiple titles to account for multiple condominiums—when the structure is nearly finished and ready to enter the market. Therefore, the start date of investment is ambiguous. The actual investment is made upon the beginning of construction, several months before the filing. The authors of the article compensate for this by lagging the dependent variable by one calendar year, factoring in the average time it takes to construct a multifamily structure. (b) is incorrect because using the condominium sales price data obtained from the BCAA, the authors are able to estimate expected price appreciation using an autoregressive method. (c) is incorrect because the number of units per project is accounted for by the dependent variable. During the four bursts of strata development, an increase in the size of the developments is also evident. (d) is incorrect, because the BCAA data includes the sale prices of all condominiums between 1979 and 1998, which is information that is used to create the seven-price indexes.

References

Baldi, F. (2013), "Valuing a Greenfield Real Estate Property Development Project: A Real Options Approach," Journal of European Real Estate Research 6, 186–217.

Bulan, L., C. Mayer and C. T. Somerville (2009), "Irreversible Investment, Real Options, and Competition: Evidence from Real Estate Development," Journal of Urban Economics 65, 247–251.

Mian, A. and A. Sufi (2014), "House of Debt," University of Chicago Press: Chicago, USA.

Novy-Marx, R. (2005), "An Equilibrium Model of Investment Under Uncertainty," Working paper. University of Chicago: Chicago, USA.

CHAPTER 2

Growth Management

In collaboration with Zach Pagel and Catherine Kurtz

Urban growth boundaries (UGBs) are government-imposed restrictions aimed at combatting excessive urban sprawl, or development and growth that pose a threat to rural and agricultural land. These boundaries are meant to incentivize development within certain parameters, which create denser urban areas. Understanding how UGBs affect the development of cities can provide use with insight on how government-imposed regulations can spur economic growth and prosperity. Effectively managing the growth of cities is an essential tool that urban planners use to ensure specific goals are being met within a city, and is a key concept in understanding how cities are formed and how it function.

When planning the expansion or creation of a city, urban planners may run into difficulty when attempting to target development to one specific area while hoping that price volatility does not impact that potential development. The demands of the market are constantly changing and to use them to the advantage of an ultimate urban plan requires very strategic planning. For example, the real estate market is currently growing very quickly in Dallas, Texas. How can city planners ensure that developers are not scared off by the uncertainty of future prices, and in addition, concentrate their developments in the city of Dallas, rather than expanding to outside the city borders? How can they ensure that development will keep up with demand and urbanization can grow? Christopher R. Cunningham examines these questions in *Growth Controls, Real Options, and Land Development,* using the State of Washington to show how the implementation of an UGB and Growth Management Acts (GMAs) can actually help predict demand, development, and prices in both urban and rural settings.

Cunningham (2007) researches the effects of the implementation of the UGB and the GMA around Seattle, Washington in Kings County to determine what kind of effects density restrictions have on development inside and outside of the boundary. An UGB is defined as a boundary imposed to control urban sprawl by concentrating high-density growth within the boundary and low-density growth outside of the boundary. The GMA mandated that certain areas of Washington great UGBs to separate high- and low-density development. Cunningham's paper attempts to elaborate on the subjects of growth management and real options in a manner that no other paper or research has done before. He accomplishes this by initially revealing the direct effects that the boundary has on development. Next, he explores repercussions of density restrictions and their impact, as a variable, on option value. Finally, Cunningham strives to uncover any connections between government regulations and real options in investment decisions.

Cunningham put in great effort to get an extensive set of data such to ensure that his findings are meaningful and well-supported. One of three primary sources for the data used in this paper came from records on parcels and building descriptions kept by the county assessor's office for the year 2002. Information on parcels kept in these files contain 70 indicator variables for possible features that commonly affect property values in that area. Building descriptions are just as detailed, with 30 different variables being laid out that may impact a building's value. For his second source, Cunningham explored real property transaction files from the county assessor's office. He did this to estimate house price uncertainty and forecast future prices over the coming year. Finally, he used county GIS files of parcel location, zoning, and jurisdictional boundaries.

He began his analysis of the data by attempting to define the effects of the growth boundary and price uncertainty on the timing of development. This was done through taking all homes completed during and after 1985 to find that by 2002, of the 163,120 parcels that could have been developed on, 95,805 had been developed on while 67,135 remained undeveloped. Next, by looking at sales from the King County real property file, Cunningham sought to measure quality-adjusted housing prices to ultimately get an idea about forecasting prices and price uncertainty in that area. After finding the total sales, dividing the county by school districts, running 1,230 separate house price regressions, estimating price uncertainty, and taking the annual average of price uncertainty term, Cunningham was ultimately able to create a mean level of price uncertainty per year per school district in the county. In total, Cunningham used a data set of over 500,000 home sales and 163,000 potential pieces of land that could be developed between 1984 and 2001.

Cunningham uses these three resources to create his own set of data that models the construction and its timing inside and outside of the UGB before and after the creation of the boundary. He additionally explores how much time passes before a piece of land is developed after the boundary is put into place. Furthermore, he looks into development site quality, changes in housing demand relative to time, and price uncertainty and future price expectations in relation to time. Using his extensive data sets, he is able to have well-supported and reliable conclusions relative to Kings County.

Cunningham's extensive research leads to credible final results from his research. He ultimately finds that in typical market situations, uncertainty leads to slower development in a particular market. However, in the presence of a GMA where higher density and urban-oriented development is encouraged, uncertainty becomes less relevant in the development process. With the GMA, comes the removal of legal development rights as long as the removal of options for landowners. When landowners do not have as many options, there is not as much uncertainty when it comes to future land development, which leads to less volatility in the market place.

Furthermore, Cunningham provides compelling evidence that the implementation of the UGB decreased development outside of the boundary in rural areas and increased development within the boundary in urban areas. The UGB then ultimately helped the GMA to achieve what it had originally been implemented to achieve.

Cunningham additionally found that after the law had been in effect, lot sizes within the boundary shrank and became denser, whereas lot sizes outside of the boundary saw enormous growth. Not only were lot sizes changing across the boundary, but also lot prices were changing so dramatically that at one point, completely empty, undeveloped lots within the UGB had higher price tags than those lots outside of the boundary that were developed.

To conclude his argument, Cunningham (2007) reasserts the fact that the Seattle area's enactment of an UGB reduced development in designated rural areas and increased construction in urban areas. Furthermore, he stresses the point that the GMA successfully removed much of the future price uncertainty and real option considerations that were preventing landowners outside the boundary from pursuing development. By taking away these barriers, the UGB only reduced development outside the border by 28 to 39 percent, a considerable difference from the 42 to 48 percent reduction that would have been seen had uncertainty surrounding future price and future use remained.

Thus, this provides an important knowledge to urban planners and policy makers in pursuing their development goals moving forward. Through using tools such as UGBs, cities can concentrate housing development in the areas that they desire, while also removing the allure for landowners outside the boundary to brush off other forms of development in hopes that their parcels may one day attract high-paying residential and multifamily developers. In the long run, this allows cities to exert control over an otherwise-free market, forcing landowners to move more quickly in developing areas that may otherwise have sat dormant for decades longer.

In addition to Cunningham's 2007 work, much other thought has been given to the idea of urban growth and the effect of government regulations such as UGBs. This includes a work by Anthony Downs (2004) of the Brookings Institution. In this book, Downs reiterates Cunningham's findings surrounding the development patterns caused by UGBs. In addition, he examines many other ways that governments can affect development, including zoning restrictions, separation of utility districts, caps on building permits, and moratoriums on construction for certain property types. Across his discussion of these policies, he also pays special attention to their impact on housing affordability, which he finds can be quite large if the policies are too restrictive or not implemented correctly. As he admits near the introduction of the book, "most growth management, growth control, and even smart growth efforts have not paid a lot of attention to providing more affordable housing," a fact that calls into question whether there is a way to address this issue while still keeping intact the many benefits that can come through policies such as UGBs.

The failure to address this question is among the several major weaknesses of Cunningham's paper. Although he incorporates many variables into his regression model that look at the type of land being developed, there is very little discussion of the type of development actually taking place on these various parcels both within and outside of the UGB. For his research to be more useful to groups such as urban planners, policy makers, and real estate developers, it would have been beneficial to include tangible examples of development projects that took place, as well as information regarding their pricing and affordability. Without this information, it is very hard for any of these groups to incorporate Cunningham's research into any sort of actionable plan.

Should Cunningham or other researchers revisit this paper as urban growth continues to rise across the United States, there are several useful actions one could take when conducting research. These include applying the research to more than just Seattle, as the findings may be drastically different in various cities. While Seattle has long been propelled by growth in the technology sector, many other cities have faced different levels of land and housing demand. In particular, an interesting example to examine would be Detroit, which saw unprecedented urban growth across the height of American auto manufacturing, and is now seeing moderate growth once again after the collapse of its dominant industry. In addition, Cunningham could also research some of the problems that come with concentrating housing growth within a particular boundary. These include items such as traffic congestion, demand for public transportation, and the increased need for educational and medical facilities. Through knowing the effect of such factors as these, governments would be much better equipped to growth policies that make the most sense for their particular communities.

Multiple Choice Questions

1. According to Christopher R. Cunningham (2007), what government interventions drove changes in development and prices in Kings County, Washington?
   a. UGBs
   b. Urban Sprawl
   c. GMA
   d. Both (a) and (c)

Explanation: Cunningham asserts that the UGB was the ultimate strategy that helped the GMA achieve what it was originally implemented to achieve. The GMA set goals, while the UGB met those goals. Therefore, both the UGB and the GMA drove changes in development and prices (amongst other changes) in Kings County, Washington. Urban sprawl is just the movement of humans away from central urban areas, so that would not make sense in the context of this article or this question.

2. According to Cunningham (2007), what is the primary purpose of an UGB?
   a. To concentrate low-density growth inside the boundary, and high-density growth outside the boundary
   b. To concentrate high-density growth inside the boundary, and low-density growth outside the boundary
   c. To create low-density growth both inside and outside the boundary
   d. To concentrate both high- and low-density growth within the boundary, and stop all growth outside the boundary

Explanation: Cunningham first explains that UGBs are primarily created to restrict where high-density growth takes place. This eliminates choice (c), which does not mention high-density growth at all. Later on, Cunningham also states that UGBs are not meant to stop all development outside the boundary, thus eliminating choice (d). This leaves the choices of which type of growth is to take place both within and outside of the boundary. As discussed throughout the paper, the purpose of the UGB is to concentrate high-density growth within the boundary, making choice (b) the correct answer.

3. According to Cunningham (2007), what is a major reason that land-owners sometimes delay development on their land?

   a. Price uncertainty

   b. Uncertainty about best use

   c. UGBs

   d. Both (a) and (b)

   e. (a), (b), and (c)

Explanation: A major portion of Cunningham's work is devoted to discussing how both price uncertainty (a) and uncertainty about the best use (b) of a parcel can delay its development. Among his main findings is that UGBs help to eliminate these uncertainties, restricting the possible uses of land and therefore reducing its potential for the price appreciation that can cause owners to "wait out" the market before pursuing development. Thus, choice (c) and by proxy choice (e) are incorrect, making choice (d) the correct answer.

References

Cunningham, C. (2007), "Growth Controls, Real Options, and Land Development," Review of Economics and Statistics 89, 343–358.

Downs, A. (2004), "Growth Management and Affordable Housing: Do They Conflict?" Brookings Institution Press: Washington, D.C.

PART II
Land Use Regulation

CHAPTER 3

Costs and Benefits of Land Use Regulation

In collaboration with James Huffman and Caroline Cromer

Land use regulations, such as zoning, ensure that certain resources are protected within communities. Creating cities with specific design features in mind is one of the essential functions of regional planning entities. Although land use regulations often serve as constructive policy solutions, they can sometimes have unintended adverse effects. It is imperative that government entities consider the broader economic implications of these regulations, and take a comprehensive cost–benefit analysis when implementing them. Understanding the positive and negative repercussions that occur as a result is important in gaining an understanding of prudent policy decisions.

Beaches have long been alluring to homeowners and a hotbed of real estate development. Coastal communities attract a wide variety of people who, in turn, impose potential dangers and harm to the area and structures surrounding beaches. Coastline development in the United States displaced a large amount of sand dune systems prior to the 1960s. The absence of sand dune systems can leave beach communities vulnerable to extreme damage from ocean storms. As understanding of the vital protection dune systems offer to the environment and structures grew over time, so did concern over real estate development practices. In 1971, the state of Florida implemented the State's Beach and Shore Preservation Act as a response to concern over increased erosion problems and beachfront real estate development. The act put Florida's Coastal Construction Control Line (CCCL) into place. The CCCL is designed to reduce overall storm damage along the Florida coast and increase the amount of open beach space available for public use. Belliot and Smith (1981) analyze the costs and benefits derived by the CCCL.

The paper is a case study done in 1981 on the costs and benefits of the CCCL program in Martin County, Florida. Martin County is located about 120 miles north of Miami on the Atlantic coast of Florida, and it was the first county for which the CCCL was incorporated. This made Martin County a reasonable choice for the study as it had the most data available to measure any impact of the legislation. Data for the study was gathered from all 353 parcels of privately owned beachfront land in Martin County. The authors assume that the government will always build at society's optimal building distance from the ocean, so no data on public sector development was included. The data on private properties was used alongside census data from 1930 to 1970 to develop a systems model of development patterns that the authors compare to the patterns they observed after the implementation of the CCCL program. Calculation of expected storm damage was done using actuarial rates published by the National Flood Insurance Program. Analysis of storm damage reduction benefits was done using data from Federal Disaster Assistance Administration grants, Small Business Administration subsidized loans, and Federal Flood Insurance claims. Calculation of administrative costs was derived from costs that were directly attributable to the Bureau of Beaches and Shores. Variance costs to riparian owners were drawn from topographic surveys. Data from other studies on coastal areas is included for the sake of comparison to the results of the Martin County study.

Belliot and Smith used a systems model of development patterns created by a modeling program from MIT referred to as DYNAMO. The model algebraically explained the connections between relevant geographic factors and identified changes in these relationships. The purpose of this model was to estimate what the patterns of development would have been had they followed the historical trends before the implementation of the CCCL. This information could then be compared to the actual data that was collected after the program was put into place. To avoid experimental error, the authors overstated the benefits of the CCCL to the public by assuming that each potential future storm would have a more aggressive impact than any past storms.

The authors found that potential recreational benefits derived from an increase in beachfront were not significant for three reasons. First, a previous study of Bay County found that very little land seaward of the CCCL was actually being developed. Second, there was a lack of demand for more public beachfront and there was an extensive amount of undeveloped beachfront that was unlikely to ever be developed. Finally, the authors concluded that there is little recreational value derived from forcing development landward, since the additional beach uncovered would still be the property of the original owner, and not available for public use other than as visual space.

The impact of the CCCL on property values along the coastline was found to be zero. To adjust for the lack of comparable home-sale data and to control for other impacts on property values, the authors measured market perceptions of the impact on the expected utility of a property before and after the implementation of the CCCL. This was determined by calculating variances among the sale prices of residential properties in Martin County. There were no significant differences among the mean adjusted price residuals that were computed for properties using regression models. This shows that there was not a change in expectations about the utility of properties after the CCCL was implemented, and that its implementation had no impact on property values.

Since the impact on beachfront property values was found to be zero, the impact on the tax base as a result of a change in property values was also found to be zero. The implementation of the CCCL might have slowed the growth of the tax base in Martin County; however, if it caused a decline in overall development activity. The authors' examination of development patterns from 1900 to 1977 found that there was a slowdown in development after the implementation of the CCCL. There was not enough evidence, however, to show that it did not come from other sources. Therefore, impact on the tax base as a result of a decrease in development activity was found to be zero, and no cost was assigned to the CCCL's impact on the tax base.

The authors run two final experiments in their paper before drawing their conclusions. The first experiment tries to find the theoretical maximum value of the CCCL by summing up the estimated costs and benefits of the line as if no development occurred prior to its implementation. This experiment found a negative net value of the CCCL for both the general public and private landowners. The hypothetical exercise indicated that there was no economic value from implementing the line since nobody received any benefits. The second experiment amortized the costs and benefits of the CCCL over a 40-year time period. The future projections were based on historic and current data on the CCCL. The experiment showed that the expected annual benefits would exceed expected annual costs only once, in the year 2027. When cumulative costs were included, there was an expected net negative benefit of the CCCL through the year 2027 and no positive benefit was projected for that time span. The cost–benefit projections in this exercise were found by subtracting administrative and private variance procedure costs from total public benefits. When cumulative costs were included, the net benefit of the CCCL was highly negative for many years and its maximum value was –$9,613 in the year 2027.

The results of the authors' study leads them to conclude that the CCCL program has no net benefit to the public or private sector of Martin County and that it should not be implemented. The authors explain that the main reason the line is not effective in Martin County is that historic development patterns have been efficient and responsible. As a result, there is little further benefit that the line can hope to achieve. Thus, the expected costs of implementing the line far outweigh the benefits.

In economics, if a policy imposes a net cost on society or a party that did not choose to have that policy implemented, it is referred to as a "negative externality." In Mian and Sufi's (2014) book "House of Debt," the authors discuss the negative effects that mortgage foreclosures had on society during the 2008 financial crisis. The lender in a mortgage bears less of the burden of a decline in property values. The majority of this burden falls onto borrowers, since it causes their equity in their homes to decline even though their mortgage loan remains unchanged. The nature of the mortgage loan industry leads to situations where a relatively isolated decline in housing values can cause all the houses in a region to decline in value—a negative externality. Similarly, in the Martin County study the public bears the negative effects of the CCCL, whereas the developers have the lowest expected costs. Therefore, the public bears the financial responsibility when the developers decide to build at nonoptimal points along the coast. Often times, these costs come in the form of externalities, and the public suffers losses paying for debris removal and disaster relief.

Although the authors found that the CCCL program was more costly than it was beneficial in both the public and private sectors, the study was performed only in Martin County, Florida. Therefore, it is difficult to apply these findings to anywhere outside of this region. In order to fully understand whether or not the program was beneficial, similar research should be done along the entire coast of Florida. So while it is impossible to know based on this study whether or not the CCCL is worth the costs in any other areas, it does suggest that the decision to implement the program should be done on a case-by-case basis.

The authors point out that this study may be unintentionally biased. This could be for two reasons. First, there was a relatively low amount of preregulation development in Martin County. The implementation of multifamily projects was primarily concentrated after the installment of the CCCL, and no significant positive changes were observed in regards to storm damage and an increase in open space. The second reason is the strength of pre-CCCL local regulations. Research shows that there was extensive local involvement in policy making dating back to 1947. As a result, the expected benefits of the CCCL were minimal because the community was already taking preventative measures to control unwanted development and discourage beach erosion prior to its implementation.

Further research on the regulations in place prior to implementing the CCCL and the degree of development in place may be able to more precisely pinpoint where the CCCL would be most effective in preventing storm damage and increasing open space. A more accurate projection of whether or not the CCCL would have any impact may reduce the costs of research because policy makers would already have a better idea of its expected effectiveness and not have to wait to observe the results only after the installment of the control line.

Multiple Choice Questions

1. According to Belliot and Smith (1981), the implementation of the CCCL was found to:
   a. Impose a net cost on both the public and private sectors in the state of Florida and should not be implemented
   b. Provide a net benefit to both the public and private sectors in the state of Florida and should be implemented
   c. **Impose a net cost on both the public and private sectors in Martin County, Florida and should be implemented on a case-by-case basis for the rest of the state**
   d. Provide a net benefit to both the public and private sectors in Martin County, Florida and should be implemented on a case-by-case basis for the rest of the state

Explanation: The authors' finding that the CCCL imposed a net cost on the public and private sectors was based on a study of properties in Martin, County, Florida, and did not use any data on properties throughout the rest of the state. The findings in Martin County, therefore, should not be used as a statement that the program is not beneficial for the rest of the state. A separate study found that the program provided a net benefit to Bay County, Florida. The authors' study as well as additional available data suggests that the application of the CCCL for any area should be determined on a case-by-case basis.

2. What are the two possible sources of bias in Belliot and Smith's (1981) study?
   a. The strength of pre-CCCL regulations and negative externalities
   b. **The strength of pre-CCCL regulations and preregulation development**
   c. Preregulation development and local involvement in policy making
   d. Negative externalities and local involvement in policy making

Explanation: Martin County, Florida had heavy pre-CCCL regulations regarding coastal development. This shows that the prevention of erosion and focus on preserving the coast was already a topic that people cared about locally prior to the study. Also, in some areas of the study there was little development prior to the installation of the CCCL. This made it difficult to observe positive changes.

3. Which of the following are negative externalities incurred by the public from the development of the CCCL that were included in Belliot and Smith's (1981) study?

   a. An increase in pollution
   b. Disaster relief
   c. Destruction of wildlife habitats
   d. Debris removal
   e. **Both (b) and (d)**

Explanation: When developers decide to build complexes at nonoptimal points along the coast, they are not the ones who are ultimately responsible for the damages that occur or the subsequent cleanup if there is a natural disaster or another incident of that nature. In the event of a hurricane, when there are properties built too close to the coast that are damaged, the public becomes responsible for the picking up of debris and disaster relief, not the company or individual who built the complex.

References

Belliot, J. and H. C. Smith (1981), "The Coastal Construction Control Line: A Cost-Benefit Analysis," Real Estate Economics 9, 367–383.

Mian, A. and A. Sufi (2014), "House of Debt," University of Chicago Press: Chicago, USA.

CHAPTER 4

The Cost of Habitat Conservation

In collaboration with James Leiva and Sadia Majid

While economic growth is often the goal when designing cities, it must be weighed against the negative externalities that urban development imposes on natural and environmental resources. Successful cities must seek to find a proper balance if the goal is to provide sustainable solutions, even if it comes at the expense of foregone economic profit. Understanding how to make these decisions is a crucial element of designing communities where people can enjoy natural spaces.

As more and more natural habitat for endangered species and those not-yet-endangered are being destroyed by urban sprawl and new development, the government and its entities are working to protect the land and the natural habitats. One of the ways that this can be done is by restricting land use and development on current agricultural lands to prevent the spread of urbanization and the subsequent destruction of the habitats on the land. The goal of these initiatives is to proactively act to ensure that the land and its inhabitants are protected and preserved. However, these actions to protect the habitats don't come without significant cost. Critics of these programs state that they are inefficient and not as effective as they should be: They believe that the cost for such environmental protection vastly outweighs the benefits and that they prevent natural growth and progress. Lovell and Sunding (2001) explore this idea and attempt to quantify the value of land that is encumbered with preexisting voluntary restrictions on development.

Lovell and Sunding (2001) seek to analyze how preexisting development restrictions affect the cost of protecting habitat through the creation and development of an econometric model and conceptual framework. The authors conduct their research using a case study of preserving vernal pools in Sacramento County, California though the restriction of development on agricultural land. Protecting endangered species and their habitats is an important duty for governments. To do this, restrictions often have to be made on the use of private land. Any restrictions set forth by the government or its entities on private property are often highly contested and questions are raised about the actual benefits compared to the real costs. It is estimated that 80 percent of endangered species have at least some part of their habitat on private land and then 50 percent of endangered species exist solely on private land (National Heritage Institute 1998.) It is often very difficult to try and measure the costs associated with restricting private land use in order to protect the environment and the habitats of endangered species. The differential property tax assessment of agricultural land has proven to make this analysis significantly more difficult and complex. A differential property tax assessment is a decrease in taxes that farmers and agricultural landowners must pay. The decrease in taxes comes from how the land is valued. With this program, the value of land is assessed using the agricultural-use value rather than the market value. The goal of these differential assessments is to lower operating expenses for farmers so that they have a better chance of staying in business. Lovell and Sunding (2001) try to develop a model and framework for how to estimate the cost to protect habitats on private land when the land is already encumbered with a voluntary agreement for a restriction on development.

Lovell and Sunding (2001) collected data using the Sacramento County Assessor's Office to search for and compile data on agricultural parcels to analyze their assessed value, sale dates, prior enrollment with development restriction legislation, soil type, and other similar metrics. The date of sale for the parcels ranged from 1975 to 1999. U.S. Geological survey (USGS) topography maps and the assessor's parcel maps were also used to better understand the actual locations and the characteristics of the land for each parcel. The location and information on the vernal pool habitats came from Sacramento County's databases. For the study, 143 sites were chosen that represented 13,902 acres of the vernal pool habitat (California Department of Conservation 1992.)

The hedonic model was constructed to analyze the impact that preexisting voluntary development restrictions had on agricultural land values. The model looked at three categories: "Prohibit," "Enrolled," and "Nonenrolled," and then included the individual variables of acreage, proximity to a roadway, water, soil quality, slope of the land, if it was in Sacramento, urban land, other land, and then Time and Time.[2] The authors used this regression model as an attempt to predict what the cost of restrictions would be to protect the vernal pools. The model predicts the expected cost to the landowner by taking the expected market value of the land minus the value of the land with restricted use. The economic intuition behind the model is that the prior voluntarily encumbered land would be worth less than similar land without the development restrictions.

The results from the data of the hedonic regression show that the further away from the center of Sacramento, the lower the property values for all three variables (enrolled, nonenrolled, and restricted). This makes sense from a fundamental real estate and economics thought process. This principle can be explained by the Bid Rent Curve that dictates that the further away from the central business district or center of the city, the lower the value of a specific parcel of land. Differences in value began to become more evident as the model progressed through the data. For example, neighborhood effects were significant in all three variables but significant in different directions. Values for agricultural land nearby to urban areas were higher for the unrestricted land and lower for the encumbered land. This could be attributed to the potential for expansion of the urban area and the unrestricted agricultural land providing the best use, compared to the restricted land. When calculating the cost of the restrictions on the land, the paper first creates a scenario where all of the land in the study is restricted and then derestricted and open for development. The data suggests that if all of the land was restricted, the aggregate value would be $32.3 million and if it were unrestricted the aggregate value would be $75.6 million, a significant difference. On a per-acre basis, the average unrestricted land plot would be worth $4,390, whereas the average restricted land plot would trail drastically at only $361 per acre (Lovell and Sunding 2001).

Lovell and Sunding (2001) use their hedonic model to conclude that it is beneficial to protect the natural habitats even if it means incurring costs to do so. They conclude that to sustain and conserve the biodiversity and the endangered species, safeguarding the environment and rare ecosystems is essential and should be government and other entities' first priority. Lovell and Sunding (2001) have justified their conclusion by showing that after analyzing the data from their case study on the vernal pools in Sacramento County, effective results were found. However, regulating or limiting the usage of private land does put a burden or enforces an extra charge on taxpayers and landowners. Thus, Lovell and Sunding (2001) attempt to establish a model to weigh the expenses of development restrictions on agriculture land with preexisting voluntary restriction. They intend to prove to the entities that the actual costs of protecting habitat or land are currently overestimated. Lovell and Sunding (2001) also imply that overlooking or disregarding these restrictions severely prejudices the economic expenses of environmental preservation on private land. Policy makers, thinking of different preservation alternatives, turn to practices such as conservation easements, the Williamson Act (the California Land Conservation Act of 1965), or others like urban planning and zoning. The Williamson Act protects land by preventing development or a change in use for agricultural land in exchange for property tax relief for the owners. The authors highlight the importance of evaluating the productivity or effectiveness of the environmental regulation when doing a cost–benefit analysis. Also emphasized is the importance of how knowing and understanding the real costs associated with such restrictions.

Lovell and Sunding (2001) examine the impact that preexisting land use restrictions have on the costs associated with protecting natural habitats in Sacramento County, California. In an article in the Missouri Law Review titled *Differential Assessment and Other Techniques to Preserve Missouri's Farmlands*, Mark Lapping, Robert Bevins, and Paul Herbers analyze the viability of various actions and public policies to protect farmland in Missouri. While Lovell and Sunding (2001) predominantly focus on cost, Lapping, Bevins, and Herbers (1977) study the viability of differential assessment and other techniques such as: zoning, fee simple purchase and leaseback, development rights acquisition, transferable development rights, land trusts, and agricultural distracting have in protecting agricultural land. Lapping, Bevins, and Herbers (1977) find that the differential assessments are at their most useful when agricultural land is at a close proximity to new developments. Agricultural land far away from new development and areas of population growth did not see as much of an influence on land values from the differential assessment. This is attributed to the fact that most states, and Missouri specifically, generally assess agricultural land at a lower rate than nonagricultural land through use-value legislation. As a result, agricultural land that is a significant distance away from new development does not see such a drastic increase in land prices as that agricultural land in close proximity to new developments, minimizing the effects of having a differential assessment in place. The authors find that if the main goal of differential assessments and tax deferral is to influence land use, it is not a very successful method. They find that the costs associated with differential assessments often outweigh the benefits and when municipalities and states are considering implementing one of these programs, they often underestimate the actual costs (decrease in tax base) of such programs. As a suggestion for a solution, the authors state that comprehensive planning must first begin at a state level to identify specific areas of concern and then continue down to the local level with efficient planning and land use controls to protect specific at-risk land locations.

There are a few weaknesses present in Lovell and Sunding (2001); for instance, the main basis of their hypothesis is to understand and explain that the cost of exploiting habitats through new development is more detrimental than preserving them, is based on two incorrect biases. First, they assume that there are a limited and small number of land tracts that are encumbered by preexisting development restrictions, tending to make this a cheaper option for landowners. Second, the authors assume that the costs associated with protecting the land will automatically lower if a permanent or provisional restriction that ensures the prevention of converting agriculture land exists. However, these biases may not be applicable for every parcel of land or to land in other areas or locations with unique sets of attributes. This fails to show that the costs of such environmental protection are more beneficial than costly. Third, the results are based on a case study with monitored and controlled variables; potentially creating differing results and conclusions than what was found in this research by Lovell and Sunding. Thus, it does not seem like a viable option to use this model on a more widespread basis. Finally, the presence of the differential property tax assessments make calculating the costs associated with preservation and value of land much more complex and difficult, limiting the usefulness of the model. Therefore, this method may not seem desirable or useful by the government or other entities. Also as per Lovell and Sunding (2001), initially, it had been observed that policies like conservation easements and others similar that dictated private land use appeared to be a good option and was capable of producing positive results. However, as time has passed, the number and size of many land trusts has increased along with their in-alliance and influence with the government. This trend diminished the usefulness of such policies as certain groups were taking advantage of the situation. This is common in most cases when speaking about large national organization that receive substantial federal funding by leveraging their power to influence land use for their own profit maximization. Furthermore, having only been focused on the area of Sacramento County, this model may not function as desired in other geographic locations. Also, the effectiveness of the hedonic model could vary in the future when considering the potential legal, economic, and political climate and as this has not been thoroughly discussed in Lovell and Sunding (2001), the future viability of the model can be questioned.

A few suggestions to improve the future research for this topic could entail applying the hedonic model to different geographic regions that have conditions that are different from Sacramento County to assess if their theory still stands. They could apply this model to other areas with vernal pools other than Sacramento County to establish generalizability and determine how results differ across different counties using the hedonic model and method. Also, the authors could consider doing longitudinal studies in the same area to observe the effects over time and assess hedonic model's effectiveness in the long run. Lovell and Sunding (2001) could also try to make their hedonic model more comprehensive, and easier to calculate by substituting elements such as differential property tax assessment with other common assessments. Ideally, improving the process of assessing the usefulness of government policies to estimate the costs of regulations and measuring and evaluating their efficiency.

Multiple Choice Questions

1. According to Lovell and Sunding (2001), which policy can government agencies use to ensure privately owned land jointly produces
   economic goods and environmental amenities?
   a. **Conservation easement**
   b. Prohibiting use of parcels
   c. All of the above
   d. None of the above

Explanation: The correct answer is (a): conservation easement. (b) is incorrect because according to Lovell and Sunding (2001) we can achieve
environmental goals without restricting the use of parcels entirely with
the help of environmental features. Thus, (c) is also incorrect. According to Lovell and Sunding (2001), privately owned land can simultane-
ously produce economic goods and environmental amenities. In such
situations, the government needs to specify environmentally acceptable
current and future uses of the property and to make sure that the landowner adheres to those uses. There are several alternative policies available
to government agencies to control the use of private land. Conservation
easements are an example of such a policy.

2. According to Lovell and Sunding (2001), generally, environmental
   protection is assured by acquisition of private land. However, in case
   of vernal pools such an extreme strategy is not required because:
   a. They are protected or commissioned by Sacramento County
   b. **Agricultural production and urban development do not cause any
      destruction in case of vernal pool**
   c. Mitigation protects them
   d. Where they exist now, protection of vernal pools is compatible be-
      cause of current land use at those locations

Explanation: The correct answer is (b): Agricultural production and
urban development do not cause any destruction in the case of vernal
pools. As per Lovell and Sunding (2001) usually environmental protection is assured by the outright acquisition of private land. Because the
vernal pool is not located in this particular region, this strategy is not
necessary. Instead the government can get a partial interest in the parcels
where vernal pool occurs. Under the terms of such an agreement, the

government would purchase from the landowner the right to alter land use in the future. A restriction on any future development would impact the market value of a property if the property has some realistic, alternative future use. The existence of such property tax incentive programs may have an empirically significant effect on the cost of development restrictions.

3. According to Lovell and Sunding (2001), what factors should land values be influenced by?

   a. Variables related to locational and geographic characteristics
   b. The expected price appreciation
   c. **Those variables that determine a parcel's profitability in agriculture and the profitability for future urban development**
   d. Those variables that determine the agricultural income

Explanation: The Answer is (c): Those variables that determine a parcel's profitability in agriculture and the profitability for future urban development. In this paper, Lovell and Sunding (2001) clearly state that two types of factors, those that determine a parcel's profitability in agriculture, and those that determine profitability for future urban development should influence land values. Soil quality, slope of the land, the presence of water, and the parcel's size all affect agricultural income. The variables that influence future urban use, and thus the unrestricted value of a parcel, are the distance from urban centers, surrounding land uses, and access variables such as road frontage, slope of the land, and number of acres.

References

California Department of Conservation (1992), "Farmland Mapping and Monitoring Program. Sacramento County Important Farmland Map 1990," California Department of Conservation: Sacramento, California.

Lapping, M., R. Bevins and P. Herbers (1977), "Differential Assessment and Other Techniques to Preserve Missouri's Farmlands," Missouri Law Review 42, 369–408.

Lovell, S. and D. Sunding (2001), "Voluntary Development Restrictions and the Cost of Habitat Conservation," Real Estate Economics 29, 191–206.

Natural Heritage Institute (1998), "Optimizing Habitat Conservation Planning on Non-Federal Lands," Natural Heritage Institute: San Francisco, CA.

CHAPTER 5

A Budgetary Framework for Housing Development

In collaboration with Kevin Sharpe and Jacob Sojka

A key policy objective of government entities is the creation of affordable housing for low-income families. It is clear that when low-income communities flourish, the spillover effects create gains for everyone. Understanding the measures that governments can take to alleviate severe poverties in certain communities gives us important insights on how we can develop cities that foster environments ripe for social mobility and prosperity.

The housing industry embodies one of the largest sectors in the United States economy. Currently, the housing sector represents roughly 15 percent of the annual GDP for the United States. In addition, roughly 40 percent of a consumer's monthly expenditure is related to housing. Furthermore, on average, the equity in a homeowner's primary residence consists of 28 percent of the total family's assets. These statistics illustrate how significant and vital the housing market is to the United States' economy.

Because the housing market is a major component to the U.S. economy, the federal government demonstrated their commitment to the housing market by undertaking four main objectives: assisting lower income families in occupying safe and clean housing, stimulating housing production, assisting in the building and maintaining of neighborhoods and communities, and increasing the number of families that own their own home. The government allocated a significant portion of the annual U.S. budget to achieving these goals. However, the Congressional Budget and Impoundment Act of 1974 was instituted and stated that any budget allocations and tax expenditures must be structured to accomplish specific housing goals and missions. As a result, how can one identify which specific budget allocations and tax expenditures solve certain problems? The goal of Solomon's (1977) paper is to attempt to provide a "budgetary framework for housing, housing finance, and community development in response to those Congressional budgetary requirements" (Solomon 1977, p. 148). Solomon's framework highlights which government strategies will address certain housing goals or missions.

In Solomon's (1977) budgetary framework, several key variables were used. The first set of variables are all problems dealing with housing consumption and housing construction. The second set of variables are housing policies utilized to attempt to solve the housing construction and housing consumption issues. Solomon measures the effectiveness of the housing strategies by stating if they sometimes, usually, or never impact a certain problem. This framework allows the government to form a coordinated plan to alleviate housing inefficiencies with approaches that have been proven to solve those specific inadequacies. The variables and results will further be explained later in this paper.

To understand how the framework works, we must analyze the issues of the national housing policy. These problems are broken down into two categories which are housing construction problems and housing consumption problems. The production problems are the overall level of housing construction, the cyclical instability in residential construction, and the availability and cost of mortgage credit and other construction factors. The overall level of housing construction is vital to the economy because the construction rate and household formation rate must mirror each other to ensure that there is an appropriate level of housing. If a proper amount of housing construction is not maintained, the housing prices will become inflated and unemployment rates in the construction industry will rise. The second production problem deals with the cyclical instability of housing construction. It is commonly agreed that restrictive credit conditions are one of the primary reasons for the volatility in housing construction. When credit availability becomes more constrictive, the level of construction will decrease. Furthermore, the level of construction unemployment has an inverse relationship to the level of housing construction. As a result, when the amount of credit available deteriorates, the level of housing construction will fall and the level of construction unemployment will rise. The last problem associated with production is the adequate supply of mortgage credit and other production factors such as land, workers, and building materials. As stated above, when there is credit restraint in the economy, interest rates will rise, and the availability of capital for the purchase and construction of homes will fall. This credit availability will have an inverse relationship on employment. As the amount of credit available decreases, the unemployment rate will increase.

The housing consumption problems are the excessive housing costs, the extent of substandard shelter, and declining and slum neighborhoods. The first consumption problem that we will address here will be excessive housing costs. Housing expenses became much more onerous than they had previously before in the time period of 1974 to 1976. In order to test the number of households who were encountering housing affordability issues, an examination was conducted to see how many households were paying over 25 percent of their annual income to housing. After the test concluded, it was found that 5.5 million households fell into the category of excessive housing costs. Most of these households were low- and moderate-income households. Second, many households also demonstrated a diminishing ability to pay their housing expenses. This was mainly due to an appreciation home values which led to higher operating expenses, property taxes, utilities, and capital costs. The second consumption issue Solomon (1977) highlighted is substandard and overcrowded housing. A property is considered to be substandard if there are no plumbing facilities or the property exhibits a degree of dilapidation. A property would be considered dilapidated if the property is a danger to the health and safety of its occupants or lacks basic plumbing features. If a property is to be classified as overcrowded, there are two metrics to determine if the property is in fact overcrowded. If there are more than 1.01 persons per room then the property would be classified as overcrowded. If the property has more than 1.51 persons per room, then the property is considered to be severely overcrowded. After reviewing the 1970 Census of Population, it was determined that 6.9 million households live in substandard shelter, and 700,000 households lived in overcrowded housing. The last consumption problem addressed is the slums and an unsuitable living environment. A slum is commonly described as a neighborhood that has experienced increasing vacancies in commercial zoned properties, dissatisfactory school districts, and a high focus of poverty and substandard homes. Furthermore, there are several potential theories for how neighborhoods develop into slums and also many different ways for dealing with these unfortunate neighborhoods.

Solomon (1977) next discusses how the federal government has gradually implemented various methods in order to combat these issues. These approaches have been broken down into five distinct categories as follows: mortgage credit and thrift insurance, housing assistance, community development support, tax expenditures, and off budget credit market activities. The first program designed by the federal government is the mortgage credit and thrift insurance activities. This platform was created to increase the consistency and stability of the mortgage credit market. The second program is Community Development, which helps improve neighborhood infrastructure and regentrify neighborhoods through grants and other sources of capital. The third budget strategy is the Housing Assistance Programs. This aims at giving less fortunate households a chance to have a higher standard of housing at a reduced expense. The last on-budget policy is the Tax Expenditure, which is when tax benefits are given such as deductions or exemptions in order to induce construction and increase capital availability to the housing market. Finally, there is one off-budget policy called Housing and Mortgage Credit Programs. This strategy is very similar to others in that it aims to increase and stabilize the mortgage credit market and stimulate construction. However, it primarily focuses on making these opportunities more attainable for the elderly and disabled.

Now that the five housing instruments and six problem areas have been established, the single budget framework that was developed by Arthur P. Solomon will now be discussed. In that framework, each government program identified above is analyzed to see if the platform will sometimes, usually, or never have an impact on any of the six housing construction and production problems. This framework is able to determine which policy instrument can be applied in order to solve a specific issue most effectively.

After analyzing the Solomon's (1977) framework, there appear to be several favorable results. Community development programs have been utilized in order to generate the development of sustainable neighborhoods and regentrify older neighborhoods that could potentially be classified as slums or dilapidated housing. For example, block grants have been instrumental in updating the infrastructure of communities and dilapidated housing structures. Furthermore, housing assistance programs are employed to stimulate new construction or restoration of subsidized price housing for lower income households. The Section 8 housing program is responsible for subsidizing rent to make the rent expenses more affordable for lower income households. Finally, real estate tax expenditures have also been largely beneficial, as tax exemptions and deductions have lowered the cost of housing, making it more affordable for lower income households, and have improved the supply of mortgage credit for the overall housing market.

Overall, Solomon's (1977) framework helps identify which programs will solve definite housing inadequacies. The benefits listed above are key examples that show the relation between fixing specific housing inefficiencies and exact government policies. By adhering to this framework, it will significantly advance the planning process associated with the housing development, urban development, and community development.

Even though Solomon's (1977) framework provides a great foundation for adhering to the legislation, there are some possible uncertainties that exist. The first uncertainty would be about the degree or the size of the impact that a certain strategy will have on any of the problems. Since there are always multiple government and private approaches being used at one point in time, it is impossible to discover the independent effect that a particular policy will have on one issue or several issues. Furthermore, it is often that these policy instruments will affect several problems all at once. However, it may in fact be more beneficial to the whole economy if the program were to focus on improving one specific issue. Another potential weakness to the model would be that, when one strategy is implanted to solve a certain problem, an additional problem is generated in the process from the implementation of the program. In addition, some policy instruments will have different effects than were anticipated. Also, housing markets located all over the United States are heterogeneous, and, as a result, policy implementations in one market may not have the desired effects that they produced in a different market. Finally, there is often a delay between the time when a program receives a budget allocation and the time when the strategy actually impacts the desired group of households. Even though this framework has many potential benefits in planning the budgetary process, the several uncertainties listed above cannot be ignored.

When thinking of ways to further investigate this foundation of research, two ideas seem to be very apparent. The first idea would be to see how the different government programs affect each other. In order to decide which program would be the best to implement moving forward, it is important to know how a mixture of certain government policies would affect the results of the housing market altogether. Second, studies should be conducted to see which government implementation strategies would be the most successful in different geographic regions and different cities. This data will be important to see if there are certain trends in certain geographic regions or in different sized cities.

Multiple Choice Questions

1. According to Solomon (1977), which of the following is NOT a reason the policy and budget decisions are so ambiguous?
   a. Often time an attempt is made to design one housing program to solve several problems; however, this can often times reduce the efficiency and impact of the solution
   b. **Programs effects are often times very anticipated resulting in the less dynamic outcomes and therefore less useful data**
   c. Programs are oftentimes combined to have a larger impact on a single problem, and this makes it difficult to assess the independent effect of the specific bundled programs
   d. The time period associated with many programs is often very long, resulting in the shift of resources and program operations before the full effect can be assessed
   e. Housing problems and markets differ across the country, meaning one effective program for an existing problem may not translate results to another housing market

Explanation: The correct answer is (b). All of the following are reasons the policy and budget decisions are indirect except for (b). Program effects often times provide much unanticipated results, providing unwanted/

lesser needed effects from chosen programs. This creates a problem because for example if a program is aiming to reduce mortgage interest payments to marginal homeowners, the result may be that only high-income home-owners benefit and the program is wasted on helping those not in need.

2. According to Solomon (1977), which of the following statements concerning the cyclical instability of housing construction is false?
   a. In the short run, there is often an overutilization of plant and construction equipment due to wide-scale bankruptcies among home-builders and real estate developers, causing them to use up their resources at less efficient rate
   b. In the long run, due to wide fluctuations in production the home-building industry becomes less efficient
   c. In the long run, to avoid the high costs of uncertain demand, the industry invests more in manpower training in order to feel more confident about providing higher job security
   d. Because more housing is built-in during the peak of the demand cycle, homebuyers have to pay much of the premium, which is in effect, instability insurance
   e. **Both (a) and (c) are false**

Explanation: The correct answer is (e). (a) is false because when there is wide-scale bankruptcies among homebuilders and real estate developers, the raw material like plan and construction equipment is NOT utilized. Prices are much higher in the less stable industry. (c) is false because instead of investing in more manpower training to provide more job security, the industry adopts higher restrictive industrial relations rules. Meaning, the industry adapts to higher government control to increase their confidence in job security, rather than actually investing in training that could lead to a more efficient workforce.

3. According to Solomon (1977), Substandard and Overcrowded Housing is defined as followed:
   a. Concentration of poor residents, by substandard shelter, and by declining or vacant commercial space
   b. Absence of plumbing facilities and the degree of dilapidation

   c. Any dwelling in a dilapidated condition that endangers the health
      and safety of occupants or lacks private toilet, bath, or hot running
      water
   d. A thickly populated, run-down, squalid part of a city, inhabited by
      poor people
   e. **(b) and (c)**

Explanation: The correct answer is (e). The Department of Housing
and Urban Development and the Bureau of the Census together defined
"Substandard" as the absence of plumbing facilities and the degree of
dilapidation. The HUD report *You and your Housing* defined substandard
housing as "any dwelling in a dilapidated condition that endangers the
health and safety of occupants or lacks private toilet, bath or hot running
water." Both (b) and (c) are correct. The main problem with a definition
like this is that many time structural deficiencies such as performance of
a heating system or the safety of an electrical system are not considered in
the official estimates. Therefore, many substandard units are not counted
or considered as substandard.

References

Solomon, A. (1977) "A National Policy and Budgetary Framework for Housing
   and Community Development," AREUEA Journal 5, 147–170.
Mian, A. and A. Sufi (2014), "House of Debt," University of Chicago Press:
   Chicago, USA.

PART III

Mixed Housing Development and Neighborhoods

CHAPTER 6

Racial Patterns

Join work with Brady Cassidy and Kate Pettinger

The Civil Rights Movement in the 1960s was campaign that vastly helped fix racial inequalities that had been prevalent in the United States for hundreds of years. However, in the late 1970s, pundits began asking questions about racial segregation, and if discrimination had truly been eliminated in all facets of society. It had not yet been a decade since the 1968 Fair Housing Act had been signed into law, and many scholars were wondering if empirical evidence could prove that positive changes in racial segregation and discrimination had been made. Examining these concerns through the lens of racial distribution as impacted by new housing construction is imperative when considering the policy goals of creating equitable cities that close disparity gaps that exist in communities of color.

In his 1977 paper, *Impact of New Housing Construction on Racial Patterns*, Erber seeks to discover if the highly projected number of new housing starts will impact urban and suburban racial patterns in a significant way in the coming years, given that there has been a little reduction in housing segregation since the Civil Rights Movement, a movement that sought to end all racial discrimination in America. Motivation for this goal was brought about by two new factors that were anticipated to heavily change the relationships affecting upward racial mobility: (1) the existence of, as previously mentioned, the federal fair housing law signed in 1968 and (2) the sharp increase within the past decade of minority households with income in the professional, mechanical, and managerial ranges (Erber 1977, p. 314). In light of these factors, Erber seeks to analyze minority access to new housing developments, as well as the impact on their access to "filtered units" in moving chains initiated by new housing starts. Filtered units, in this context, describe housing units that are made available via moving chains. A filtered unit is a unit whose previous tenants immigrated to a newer, and presumably nicer, unit, paving the way for other, presumably poorer, tenants to move into the abandoned unit. This starts a chain of moving, and these chains are usually initiated by the construction of new residential properties. This is an important concept to grasp, as Erber refers to filtered units and moving chains often throughout his paper.

Erber used several metrics in his analysis of new housing construction's impact on racial distribution. He first cites an index created by a researcher named Karl Taeuber, which shows that 99 out of 109 cities analyzed by Taeuber and his associates experienced a decrease in segregation between whites and blacks over the 10-year span of 1960 to 1970 (see Sorensen *et al.*, 1974). Important to note in this index is that ten cities' segregation index actually increased, despite the Civil Rights Movement being in full swing. Erber notes, however, that Taeuber only examined segregation in central cities and not the suburbs, which were expanding heavily at the time.

Erber also examines the median incomes for black and white households in the late 1960s and early 1970s. Although blacks' median annual income rose by 31 percent between 1965 and 1970, it subsequently dropped by 2.1 percent from 1970 to 1974. However, despite the overall absolute increase in blacks' income, Erber points out that, in the competitive and segregated housing market, an increase in *absolute income* for blacks holds less significance in determining their ability to compete for housing than an increase in their *relative income* to whites, their primary competitors. This is an important distinction, because in contrast with blacks' median annual income, whites' income increased by 2.7 percent between 1970 and 1974 (Erber 1977, p. 325). Black median income is, on average, only about 60 percent of white median income (Erber 1977, p. 326).

Another data metric that Erber examines involves Standard Metropolitan Statistical Areas (SMSAs), which are simply urban areas considered representative of the majority of metropolitan areas in general. He cites a study conducted by the U.S. Bureau of Census, showing that the percent of black households in 1974 that occupied units built between 1970 and 1974 is much higher than it was in 1956.

The last piece of data that Erber examines in his analysis is an index constructed by the National Committee Against Discrimination in Housing (NCDH) in 1970. The index lists 46 selected housing marketing areas, and rates them on criteria including: existing patterns of segregation, minority income, educational level, automobile ownership, and characteristics of housing occupied by minorities. This index was used to measure the probability of minority homeseekers responding to housing opportunities away from current racial concentrations; a higher score indicates that the corresponding metropolitan area would have a higher probability of success in marketing newly built housing units to minorities *away* from the outstanding racial concentrations. Erber was able to conclude from the index, by comparing the individual scores of all 46 housing areas, that "newly constructed housing occupied by blacks is likely to have no impact on racial patterns, or an effect that is minimal, incremental, and marginal." (Erber 1977, p. 328)

Of crucial importance in examining this data and understanding its impact on racial distribution is the comprehension of the contemporary city, a phenomenon that has appeared and become common since the industrial revolution. Erber notes that industrialization and urban development, while not necessarily codependent, are highly correlated. Industrialization's need for manpower created a ". . .vortex that drew itself humanity from far and near" (Erber 1977, p. 317). Immigrants moved to these developing urban areas by the thousands, renting cheap, inner city units from where they could easily access their place(s) of employment. In his analysis, Erber brilliantly describes the nature of the contemporary city: "The city's vortex, unlike nature's, plunged the newcomer in at the center and moved him outward by successive stages. As economic growth propelled him upward socially, the urbanization process drew him outward spatially. He passed through houses previously occupied by others on their way upward and outward. The ultimate goal was a newly constructed house at the city's edge. . ." (Erber 1977, p. 318). This goes to show that, historically speaking, inner city housing units were filtered, cheap, and generally for people of lower socioeconomic status, while peripheral housing units (i.e., suburbs) were new, expensive, and indicative of wealth and superior social status.

The results of Erber's analysis confirmed the concerns that were being manifested by scholars: racial distribution has made marginal progress in the 10 years since the Civil Rights Movement. Blacks, centrally located in cities (as the historic nature of the contemporary metropolis predicts), were still limited in their access to new housing starts, relative to whites. New housing developments were primarily taking place in the suburbs, while blacks were primarily living in inner cities. Expensive suburban houses were not conducive to black tenants, whom on average had 60 percent of the median income of whites. As a result of this disparity, blacks' main pathway away from the central city is through filtered houses that were previously inhabited, instead of a new housing unit. This does not fix the discrepancies in racial distribution, and whites and blacks are still segregated, even if it is over larger geographical areas. In addition to these results, Erber's review of survey compliance tests, conducted by select fair housing groups from 1970 to 1976, revealed that flagrant disregard for the law was still widespread (Erber 1977, p. 322), indicating that newly constructed housing laws for racial minorities has not been assured by the mere passage of the law.

It is from these results that Erber concludes racial distribution in America still has a long ways to go before it can be considered fully integrated. He predicts that blacks will continue to live in cities for many years to come, and blacks' income relative to whites' is a significant limiting factor. Erber concludes that new housing starts have had a very limited, if not insignificant, effect on racial distribution in the contemporary cities of America, despite nearly a decade having passed since the Civil Rights Movement and the passage of the federal fair housing law.

One of the weaknesses of Erber (1977) was that it really only examined developing urban areas, and didn't expand its scope beyond the suburbs of select major cities. If perhaps Erber had expanded the parameters of the study, trends may have been noticed in other parts of the United States. The cities used were seemingly picked arbitrarily, as their qualifying attributes were not enumerated to the reader. It is possible that a more random sample, of a larger sample size, would have yielded statistically different results than what were presented.

It would be very interesting to have a similar analysis done today in 2015, nearly 40 years later. A prospective scholar could perhaps examine the largest city in each of the 50 states, and analyze whether racial distribution has made significant progress or remained a part of the contemporary American city. A suggestion is to examine more than just the disparity of blacks and whites: involving other races and ethnicities as well could provide fascinating insight into modern day segregation and even possibly discrimination in evolving American cities.

Multiple Choice Questions

1. According to Erber (1977), filtered housing can be best described as:
   a. Housing where landlords rigorously screen tenants before offering leases
   b. Housing made available through "moving chains" initiated by housing starts
   c. Housing that undergoes inspection from a federal housing agency
   d. A housing practice that slows urban growth and development

Explanation: The correct answer is (b): Housing made available through "moving chains" initiated by housing starts. Filtered housing is a term that describes a house that essentially is "not new." For example, say a middle-class family's income is doubled due to a promotion at work. This family, with increased income, decides to build a new house. They pick a spot in the suburbs with available land, build the house, and move. Their previous house is vacant, and considered "filtered." A family from the inner city, coincidentally, has also just received an increase in their disposable income. They decide to move to the recently vacated "filtered" house, and a chain of moving "upward socially and outward spatially" has begun.

2. According to Erber (1977), how is the contemporary city most like a "reverse vortex" in nature?
   a. Immigrants rent houses on the outskirts of the city and slowly migrate inwards
   b. The wealthy elite rent inner-city units before slowly migrating outwards

c. **It put the newcomer at the center and moved him outward by successive stages**

d. The modern city was considered harmful to economic productivity

Explanation: The correct answer is (c): It put the newcomer at the center and moved him outward by successive stages. Erber (1977) likened a contemporary city to the opposite of a natural vortex (like can be witnessed in bodies of water). In a natural vortex, things are captured by the outward-most forces/arms of the vortex and slowly dragged inwards toward the eye. In the contemporary city, it is the opposite: the "newcomer" (immigrant) is started right in the middle (inner city) so that he can work at his industrial/manufacturing job. As time goes on, he elevates his socio-economic status (by working/increasing income) and can afford to move into nicer, newer houses that are being built on the outskirts of the city, due to the economic and geographical expansion of the urban area.

3. According to Erber (1977), why was racial distribution in urban areas slow to improve, despite heavy economic growth?

   a. **New houses were built in the suburbs, while blacks lived in the inner city**

   b. Blacks lived in the suburbs, while new houses were built in the inner city

   c. Whites' median income, relative to blacks', was very low

   d. Recurring natural disasters stunted economic growth and development

Explanation: The correct answer is (a): new houses were built in the suburbs, while blacks lived in the inner city. Due to the contemporary city as described by Erber, people with low income (in the case, blacks) lived in the inner city, where housing units were cheaper and working was easier. New housing construction was primarily happening in the suburbs, as cities expanded geographically. Therefore the racial segregation persevered.

References

Erber, E. (1977), "Impact of New Housing Construction on Racial Patterns," Journal Real Estate Economics 5, 313–336.

Sorensen, A., K. Taeuber and L. J. Hollingsworth (1974), "Indexes of Racial Residential Segregation for 109 cities in the United States, 1940 to 1970," Institute for Research on Poverty, University of Wisconsin: Madison.

CHAPTER 7

Employment Growth

In collaboration with Ryan Haugland and Raquel Fernandez

Housing prices directly affect the decision individuals make when pursuing employment in certain areas. Rational actors make decisions that maximize individual benefit, which create incentives to relocate to areas where this condition is met. Understanding the role that housing prices play on the dynamics of labor migration can give us some insight on the measures policy makers can take to attract workers.

What do government spending, social security, education, and international trade all have in common? They are all controlled by the government and their regulations. In every election of a new president these are the topics that potential candidates are being asked about. These seem to be the focus of everyone's attention and tend to get the most media coverage. All these items are great for America as a whole, but do they necessarily affect each of us individually? Not substantially at least, but one area that does affect almost everyone is house pricing. This is the area that most individuals end up sinking most of their income into. This is the factor that when house prices go up people feel richer and when they go down they feel poorer. House prices drive most decisions for individuals and families, and government regulation, which may vary across locations, affect house pricing in different ways.

What are the effects of housing prices on labor migration? Raven Saks (2008) explores this important question and finds that the elasticity of house prices, which is a result of barriers to construction in certain local metropolitan markets, has a large effect on the amount of labor migration to certain areas. He also claims that places with low barriers to construction, meaning that houses can be built with hardly any frictions, will have very little change in house prices, thus making them more attractive to labor migration, whereas zones with high barriers to construction will have large upward shifts in house prices, thus making them less attractive to migrating workers.

Saks (2008) starts out by introducing several constraints that can be found when facing construction planning; one of them is Government regulation, which affects house pricing in different ways. This is a complex factor, as regulations vary from city to city, due to the fact that land use policy is controlled by local governments. To study the impact of such various policies, the author uses six different sources to show the effect of government regulations on local house prices.

On the one hand, the first source is a survey conducted by the Wharton Urban Decentralization Project in the late 1980s, one of Saks (2008) main sources, and uses questions on zoning approval and permit processing time to draw conclusions about local government housing supply regulations.

Then, the second survey was undertaken by the Fiscal Austerity and Urban Innovation project and shows how the strict limitation of growth control is being used as a tool on housing development.

Moreover, a third difficulty for construction which is faced is the preservation of historic areas; such as historic districts, singular buildings, or archaeological sites. So as to find evidence on this factor the author collects information on the amount of land used for historical reasons from the National Register of Historic Places (NRHP).

The fourth issue that is addressed in Sack's paper is how the state government also implements regulations on land for environmental reasons, or to control the development of new towns. This data is collected from a study implemented by the American Institute of Planners.

Finally, he also includes information from two surveys of local government officials concerning the overall degree of housing supply regulation in each place. The first survey is a survey of the Regional Council of Governments and the second survey is by the International City Managers Association.

The author constructs a model supposing that elasticity of housing supply is a function of regulation and other factors including some fixed effects which are: the year and the metropolitan area. Therefore, the omitted factors such as geographic amenities, which are constant over time, will not affect the estimation. Taking into account the data found on the paper, on average a 1-percent increase in labor demand is associated with a 0.25-percent increase in housing stock and a 0.8-percent increase in housing prices. The more regulation there is, the less houses that are constructed and the higher are the house prices.

Constraints on the supply of housing have an impact on local labor markets. In every metropolitan area, the marginal product of labor declines with the level of employment so that the demand for labor is downward sloping. Labor demand depends on how much output a certain city produces; for example, back in the early 90s Detroit was producing the most cars—an utopia for auto workers—but today it is in financial ruins and hardly able to keep any workers because wages are so low. On the other hand, labor supply is determined by the size of the population, which affects housing supply levels. Population varies due to several factors which are an increase in wages, decreases in house prices, and personal preferences.

An increase in labor demand causes wages to increase in a certain area. These wage increases attract workers from other regions, which causes population (labor supply) to increase; as new workers arrive in the city they need houses; therefore, they cause a rise in housing prices. In inelastic housing supply areas, the increase in house prices is greater than areas with a more elastic housing supply, because it is easier for elastic housing supply areas to construct houses, apartments, and other buildings to face the rise in housing demand for the workers who migrated. This increase in housing supply keeps house prices around the same level they were before the demand shock. All of the effects described above are short-run effects.

In the long run employment steadily rises slightly above a 1.5-percent increase and then falls to about a 1-percent increase from its initial level about 15 years after the shock. Wages decline gradually and after about 25 years return to their initial preshock level. House prices rise by roughly 2 percent at the start and stay that way for longer than all other variables, but in the end they fall below their initial level and end at a long-run equilibrium. Finally, employment effects vary between inelastic and elastic areas. In elastic areas, a 1-percent increase in labor demand leads to a 1-percent increase in employment, but in inelastic areas a 1-percent increase in labor demand only leads to a 0.9-percent increase in employment, so there is a small gap of unemployment increase.

Although the author feels his model does a more than sufficient job in showing the relationship between government regulations and housing supply, he does discuss a few problems he feels could occur while evaluating the model. First, Saks states that some of the numbers may be biased due to areas that have high constraints on other things as well and not just housing for example, employment constraints, environmental constraints, and so on. Second, weather could be a decisive factor because people would desire to live in areas that have a warmer climate, such as California. Third, the age of the metropolitan area can also affect the decision of workers because older areas tend to be less productive than newer areas. Fourth, he states that his index might be correlated with geographic factors that make the supply of housing more inelastic in some areas relative to others. Finally, he says local governments might impose stricter regulations in areas that have higher expected future demand of housing.

In conclusion, once the authors model is fully constructed it is clear to see that areas with inelastic housing supply will have higher wages, lower employment, and higher house prices and areas with elastic housing supply will have lower wages, lower house prices, and more employment. In the short run there are many effects, but in the long run house prices settle at a price below their initial value. Moreover, it is important to note that the authors model is not perfect, but it does paint a good picture of how housing supply affected house prices, employment, and wages during the financial crisis.[1]

Multiple Choice Questions

1. According to Sacks (2008), which of the following statements is false?
   a. Inelastic housing areas will have higher house prices, higher wages, and lower employment levels
   b. **Elastic housing areas will have higher house prices, higher wages, and lower employment levels**

---

[1]In contrast to Sacks' (2008) arguments however, Mian and Sufi (2014) claim that sometimes unemployed workers have less incentives to move to other locations to look for a job, due to the possibility to skip mortgage payments, which delays foreclosure and government assistance. This could explain why sometimes housing prices would not adjust to changes in labor demand and supply, because workers might be less willing to move if they have other sources of income apart from labor wage. Moreover, housing prices are also affected by several factors which are not only related to construction.

   c. Elastic housing areas will have lower house prices, lower wages, and higher employment levels

   d. It is easier to construct house in elastic areas, as opposed to inelastic areas

Explanation: The answer is (b). Elastic housing areas will have lower house prices, lower wages, and higher employment levels because they have an easier time constructing houses, thus making it easier for them to adapt to employment migration. (a) is incorrect because it is indeed inelastic housing that displays those characteristics. (c) is incorrect because that is the definition of elastic house prices. (d) is incorrect because it is easier to construct houses in elastic areas as opposed to inelastic areas.

2. According to Sack (2008), which is not a short-/long-run effect of housing supply?

   a. There is a strong relationship between an increase in labor demand and an increase in labor employment

   b. In more constrained labor supply areas, an increase in labor supply leads to higher house prices, which leads to a higher wage level and an increase in employment

   c. An increase in labor demand is also associated with higher wages, and a large significant change in house prices

   d. In the long run house prices, after a slight rise in the short run, fall below their initial level and eventually settle at a long-run equilibrium point

Explanation: The answer is (c), because in the short run there is a small/insignificant change in housing supply and not a large change. (a) is incorrect because there is a strong correlation between labor demand and labor employment. (b) is incorrect because there is a small increase in unemployment of 0.01 percent (1 to 0.9 percent). (d) is incorrect because that is a long-run effect.

3. Which of the following is a problem with the model constructed by Sack (2008)?

   a. Local governments might impose stricter regulations in areas that have higher expected future demand of housing

   b. Weather as a factor because people want to live in areas that are nicer in terms of weather

   c. The age of the metropolitan area because older areas tend to be less productive than newer areas

   d. All of the above are problems with the model

Explanation: The answer is (d) because all of the above are stated problems listed in Sack's (2008) paper.

References

Luque, J. (2014), "Wages, Local Amenities, and the Rise of the Multi-skilled City," Annals of Regional Science 52, 457–467.

Luque, J. (2013), "Heterogeneous Tiebout Communities with Private Production and Anonymous Crowding," Regional Science and Urban Economics 43, 117–123.

Mian, A. and A. Sufi (2014), "House of Debt," University of Chicago Press: Chicago, USA.

Sacks, E. R. (2008), "Job Creation and Housing Construction: Constraints on Metropolitan Area Employment Growth," Journal of Urban Economics 64, 178–195.

CHAPTER 8

Traditional Neighborhood Development

In collaboration with James LaPierre

New urbanism refers to a movement in architecture and urban planning that places increased emphasis on pedestrian and transit-oriented neighborhood design principles in an effort to create a more cohesive community. Urban planning expert William Fulton (1996) writes that the two primary goals of the New Urbanist movement are (1) to create a greater sense of community by accommodating more diversity of land uses and social interaction in neighborhoods and by rethinking the "public realm," especially public spaces and the typical streetscape,[1] and (2) to reorient the typical community toward a pedestrian and transit-friendly environment, while also minimizing negative traffic and environmental effects. The amount of new urbanist communities (also referred to as traditional neighborhood developments or TNDs) in the United States has grown from less than five in the early 1990s to over 200 by 1998. Although the number of socially conscious traditional neighborhood developments have grown exponentially, academic scholarship examining the implications of such developments on housing prices has been sparse. The goal of Tu and Eppli's (2001) research is to determine whether single-family homebuyers pay a higher price to live in new urbanist developments compared to similar homes in surrounding areas. In addition, the authors wish to determine whether this price difference is due to new features available solely to TNDs or other factors.

---

[1] See Luque (2013, 2014) for a general equilibrium approach to the formation of neighborhoods as places where individuals live and work.

To accomplish this task, authors Tu and Eppli (2001) analyzed single-family home sales transaction data from 1994 to 1997 in three neighborhoods: Kentlands, Gaithersburg, Maryland; Laguna West, Sacramento, California; and Southern Village, Chapel Hill, North Carolina. The data for the study was obtained from First American Real Estate Solutions (FARES), a reputable real estate information and analytics business. These three areas were chosen by the authors as they all can be defined as new urbanist developments and they also have proximal neighborhoods with comparable nonurbanist single-family homes. The authors provide information about the value of homes sold as well as the characteristics and features of the homes. To ensure an accurate data set, transaction data of homes with unusual or outlying characteristics such as an extremely high price or additional land were removed from the study. Combined, the authors collected pricing data on over 5,000 homes in the three geographical regions.

Tu and Eppli's (2001) primary model for analysis is the hedonic price model. The theory supporting the model is that home prices are determined as a bundle of the attributes the home contains. By examining the mean home price in each area, the authors were able to use the hedonic price model to determine to what extent each individual characteristic affects home prices. In addition to gathering sales transaction data, Tu and Eppli (2001) are able to isolate specific housing characteristics (such as lot square footage, home square footage, whether the home contains a basement or not) in an effort to determine (1) the average price of homes sold in new urbanist and conventional neighborhoods and (2) what characteristic(s) determine these prices (fireplaces, pools, building materials, etc.). The authors utilize this model and believe that it is valid because it has been used extensively in previous housing market scholarship. With this data, Tu and Eppli (2001) are able to compare price discrepancies in the average sale price of homes in new urbanist communities with similar homes in nonurbanist areas. By accounting individually for key housing attributes, Tu and Eppli (2001) are able to determine whether it is these characteristics that are causing the price discrepancies or other factors such as attributes available only to TNDs.

The results of Tu and Eppli's (2001) study confirm their hypotheses. Although there is no doubt that a price premium exists for homes in new urbanist developments, the actual amount of such a price premium differs greatly by location. The authors find that to live in the new urbanist community, homebuyers pay a premium of approximately 14.9 percent of the property value in Kentlands, 4.1 percent in Laguna West, and 10.3 percent in Southern Village. The authors propose that this variance in price premiums may be due to consumer preference differences between the areas. In addition, they also suggest that the price differences could be result of the degree in which new urbanism principles are implemented in each area. In order to ensure a fair comparison, the homes studied in the TNDs, which were all built in the 1990s, are compared with nearby homes of similar age. Despite this, the data still supports the claim that homes in new urbanist communities are more expensive than comparable homes in nearby areas. Results from the hedonic analysis indicate that housing attributes (fireplaces, pools, etc.) were not the source of the increased price of homes in TNDs, meaning that the new urbanist community price premium is simply a result of increased community planning and design. Tu and Eppli's (2001) research demonstrates that some homebuyers are willing to pay a premium to live in a more socially conscious, smart and walkable community.

The New Urbanist movement has been growing rapidly in popularity over the past few decades, as young homebuyers look to purchase homes with walkable neighborhoods, public transit systems, and more cohesive communities. By comparing the prices of single-family home sales in a traditional neighborhood development with sale prices of homes in surrounding developments, this study explores the implications of new urbanism on housing prices. To put it simply, this study determined that homebuyers consistently pay higher prices for homes in TNDs compared to similar homes in other neighborhoods. Tu and Eppli (2001) used a hedonic price model to ensure that it was not additional household features (fireplaces, pools, etc.) that caused this increase in price in TNDs, but in fact the price difference is due to the increased benefits of living in a new urbanist community.

This study conducted by Tu and Eppli (2001) would not have been possible without previous scholarship on new urbanism/neotraditional planning. William Fulton's 1996 article "The New Urbanism: Hope or Hype for American Communities?" was one of the first articles published examining

New Urbanism from an academic perspective. In the article, the author describes the history of New Urbanism and the design principles and characteristics that define the movement. While Fulton's article describes the many attributes and benefits of TNDs, Tu and Eppli's (2001) article is much more analytical in nature. However, we cannot dismiss Fulton's contribution as Tu and Eppli's (2001) article was likely heavily influenced by his work. Both Tu and Eppli and Fulton's articles complement each other well and provide novel scholarship in the field of real estate/urban economics research (see Luque 2015) for a review of recent research in this field.

Although Tu and Eppli's (2001) research was well-executed, there might be room for improvement. This study only examined three areas of the United States and one may wonder whether the results would differ if the study accounted for ten, even twenty geographical locations. For future research, one may wish to examine this question with a larger variety of areas throughout the country. In addition, an updated version of this study would be incredibly useful. This study was conducted using data from 1994 to 1997; it would be interesting to see this study done again using contemporary data. One may also wish to study the reasons behind the increased value of homes in TNDs. What is it that these communities offer and why are homebuyers willing to pay more to live in new urbanist neighborhoods? Perhaps young homebuyers who can afford higher priced homes in new urbanist communities gravitate toward them in order to reduce their carbon footprint; however, this is just one of many possible hypotheses. Tu and Eppli (2001) contribute important information regarding new urbanist home prices; however, there is much work to be done in the academic study of traditional neighborhood developments.

Multiple Choice Questions

1. What are the main results of Tu and Eppli's (2001) study?
   a. **Single-family homebuyers consistently pay more to live in homes in new urbanist communities (TNDs) compared to similar homes in conventional suburban developments**
   b. Single-family homebuyers consistently pay more to live in homes in new urbanist communities (TNDs) compared to similar homes in conventional suburban developments

    c. Single-family homebuyers should not purchase a home, as it is more cost-effective to rent a living space rather than own one

    d. Single-family homebuyers consistently pay more to live in homes in the middle of big cities compared to similar homes in rural areas

Explanation: (a) is the correct answer. Single-family home sales transaction data from the three neighborhoods studied prove that the price of homes in new urbanist communities are consistently higher than the prices of comparable homes in conventional developments as a result of features available solely to TNDs. Answers (c) and (d) are irrelevant in regards to the topic of Tu and Eppli's (2001) study.

2. According to Tu and Eppli (2001), why was data gathered from Kentlands, Gaithersburg, Maryland; Laguna West, Sacramento, California; and Southern Village, Chapel Hill, North Carolina?

    a. The authors of this article grew up in these areas

    b. All three areas contain new urbanist communities (TNDs) with comparable homes in nearby conventional neighborhoods

    c. Tu and Eppli wanted to visit these three areas so they chose to study them

    d. None of the above

Explanation: (b) is the correct answer. Tu and Eppli (2001) specifically chose to study these areas as they all feature a new urbanist development in addition to similar (comparable) homes in the surrounding area. Answers (a) and (c) are irrelevant in regards to the study.

3. What model was used in Tu and Eppli (2001) to determine the value of homes in both new urbanist and conventional neighborhoods?

    a. Poisson-lognormal model

    b. Standard, partial-equilibrium real options model

    c. Urban growth model

    d. Hedonic price model

Explanation: (d) is the correct answer. In the paper, the authors explicitly state that they used the hedonic price model to determine the value of the homes they studied. The hedonic price model isolates the effects of new urbanism from other home characteristics (building quality, features, etc.) to determine to what extent each attribute affects home cost. Neither (a), (b), nor (c) were mentioned/used in this study.

References

Fulton, W. (1996), "The New Urbanism: Hope or Hype for American Communities?" Lincoln Institute of Land Policy: Cambridge, MA.

Luque, J. (2015), Urban Land Economics, Switzerland: Springer

Tu, C. and M. Eppli (2001), "An Empirical Examination of Traditional Neighborhood Development," Real Estate Economics 29, 485–501.

PART IV

Taxes

CHAPTER 9

Impact Fees

In collaboration with Mason Engnes and Nathanial Matteson

In any market where land is utilized, there will always be interactions between the interests of private firms and those of society; short-term fixed costs, long-term debt obligations, private profits, and public externalities will be at the center of a firm's conversation with local approval agencies. Real estate developers often encounter this debate as the implicit costs of construction and higher utility requirements must either be paid for by the firm initially, or fall on the region's population over a period of time.

In their 2006 paper, "Impact fees and single-family home construction," Gregory Burge and Keith Ihlanfeldt argue that private actors should embrace impact fees by local governments as they reduce the costs associated with seeking permit approval, increasing construction completion rates, as well as increasing the demand for homes by young, moderate income, first-time home buyers. Within building permit negotiations, a strategy local governments can employ is the stipulation of impact fees alongside urban and suburban development projects. Burge and Ihlanfeldt (2006) effectively describe them as:

> "Impact fees are one-time levies, predetermined through a formula adopted by a local government unit, that are assessed on property developers during the permit approval process. They are used for the provision of public infrastructure services (such as roads, schools, parks, and other recreational areas, libraries, and water and sewer) that are necessary to adequately serve new development." (Burge and Ihlanfeldt 2006)

The thought of additional costs frustrates many developers who believe their project provides a positive enough effect on a community as to justify government expenditures on project-related infrastructure like improved roadways and power. However, Burge and Ihlanfeldt (2006) believe that having developers cover these costs pushes them to plan their projects in a more durable manner.

Their paper serves to dispute claims made by developers that impact fees produce a backward shift in housing supply and increase the price of homes, deterring low-income consumers and affordable housing construction. The Burge and Ihlanfeldt model instead maintains that impact fees, under certain circumstances, actually serve to increase housing supply and promote regional desirability among young professionals and families by reducing future property taxes. Their findings conclude that impact fees, in nonwater and sewer infrastructure projects, increase the completion percentage of all homes in "inner-suburban" areas as well as medium- and large-scale home construction in "outer-suburban" areas. This focus away from water and waste infrastructure stems from a tradition that these nonwater/sewer public utilities be financed by local property taxes (instead of user fees) and that a reduction in these costs on the household serves to increase unit demand.

Their results rely on data assembled in contact with county planning and building offices in the state of Florida where 41 of 67 counties used some sort of impact fee during the study period 1993 to 2003. For control, the data is categorized into two types: first, those infrastructure costs of services funded by users (e.g., tolls to repay the costs of bridge construction) and second, those typically funded by property taxes; the first includes water and sewer fees, the second group does not. This distinction is important for Burge and Ihlanfeldt's argument, infrastructure that is needed for development projects but cannot be funded through user fees will be especially costly for a region's taxpayers. In addition, newly constructed single-family homes are grouped by size and expected affordability to moderate income households based on 2002 average home prices: very affordable, 600 to 1500 sq/ft (averaged $106,185 in 2002); affordable, 1501 to 2200 sq/ft ($139,384); and unaffordable, 2201 to 5000 sq/ft ($228,189). To account for the influence impact fees can have on existing structures, Burge and Ihlanfeldt utilize a standard repeat-sales model that studies year-to-year housing prices alongside a cumulative price index to build a "benchmarked annual real constant-quality price index" for the date period.

Burge and Ihlanfeldt's (2006) model of housing equilibrium relies on a simple initial formula where housing prices (V), is dependent on a function of variable construction opportunity cost (C), the agricultural price of land (P_L), project approval cost put on developer (A), and two sets of impact fees, those financed by property tax (F_T) and user fees (F_U). To support their theory, the authors must illustrate that an increase in F_T or F_U increases V by decreasing A. If the change in housing price ($\triangle V$) exceeds the net change ($\triangle F - \triangle A$), we can conclude the city's growth is accelerating; if $\triangle V$ does not, the city is in decline. A limit on this model is that landowners must be compensated, such that the price of a unit of housing stock (annual rent rate, R) exceeds the cost of capital (ρ). One consideration that is important is that development projects seem to serve merely a short-term purpose and come with heightened risk over time and require infrastructure with long-term costs. This situation will be highly inefficient without impact fees. When localities are left with costly public works that were destined for failed construction projects, the residents can become alienated and prefer exclusionary barriers and these regulations increase permit costs for all firms in the area, hurting housing supply.

Using the data collected and basic supply and demand intuition, the authors apply the numbers to three models of regression analysis; a fixed effect (FE), random trend (RT), and lagged dependent (LD) variable models. For their purposes, FE is central to the generalizability of the study's broader findings to markets outside Florida and so it will be the focus. The RT and LD models are important, but lend themselves to more area-specific factors that don't explain much about the nature of impact fees. The fixed effect model dictates that the number of houses completed (C) in area (i) during period (t) are dependent on variable levels of real water/sewer impact fees (WSIF) and real nonwater/sewer fees (NWSIF) from the previous year (t–1), subject to area-specific elements (α_i) and (γ_t) as well as an idiosyncratic error term (ε_{it}).

Using this framework, the results found that impact fees increased the rate of homes completed in the fixed effects model; nonwater/sewer impact fees had a greater effect on the completion of houses than water/sewer infrastructure, in some cases, water/sewer fees actually had a negative impact on housing completions. Small-sized homes experienced less change than medium and large houses due to nonwater/sewer fees.

Looking at the data, one also sees that inner and outer suburban areas experienced different effects, depending on the size of the home. For small houses, the difference in inner and outer suburbs was miniscule, changing only 0.04 percent in inner suburbs and 0.02 percent in outer suburbs due to nonwater/sewer effects. The medium-sized homes experienced a 0.142 percent change in inner suburbs and a 0.205 percent change in outer suburbs due to nonwater/sewer effects. Large houses had a 0.228 percent change in the inner suburbs and a 0.102 percent change in the outer suburbs due to nonwater/sewer fees.

The main results of the data show that medium- and large-sized houses benefited from nonwater/sewer fees, but small-sized houses did not. It is also seen that being in an inner or outer suburb does not fully determine whether or not nonwater/sewer fees have an impact on housing completions. It has to do with both the type of suburb and size of house; however, the data does support the idea that impact fees increase housing completion and the supply of housing in the long run.

Small houses in the outer suburbs experienced no change, but in inner suburbs they experienced an 82-percent increase in completions. Medium houses that were completed experienced a 30-percent increase in inner suburbs and a 36-percent increase in the outer suburbs. Large houses experienced a 24-percent increase in the inner suburbs and a 26-percent increase in the outer suburbs in completions. All houses combined experienced a 44-percent increase in completions in inner suburbs and a 29-percent increase in completions in the outer suburbs. This goes along with their idea that nonwater/sewer impact fees increase the supply of housing. Overall there were a total of 1863 extra houses completed because of these impact fees. This gives opportunity for even more houses to be built if the ideas of impact fees being an asset can continue to grow in the minds of local governments.

Overall, the paper offers a fresh view of impact fees. Burge and Ihlanfeldt (2006) aim to persuade developers that impact fees can be beneficial by eventually increasing the supply of houses in the market by indirectly reducing project approval costs. They effectively brought light to the indirect effects impact fees have on the housing market when focused on the right projects within the state of Florida.

A related phenomenon to the study of impact fees is the discussion of banking regulation and reform after the most recent global financial crisis. The 2014 book, "House of Debt," written by Atif Mian and Amir Sufi, argues that the "Great Recession" of 2008 to 2009 was a result of a large increase in private household debt prior to 2007. This debt theory proposes that recessions are preceded by a large increase in household debt that is disproportionate to home equity. When this imbalance exists, and housing prices decline as a result of market imperfection, mortgage borrowers fall victim to a "levered losses" framework where those who take on debt are held primarily responsible for a conditions outside of their control. Burge and Ihlanfeldt (2006) believe that if developers pass impact fees onto the public, and projects result in unsuccessful construction or unprofitable businesses, then people are hurt by both higher taxes and an increased distrust of private development. Much like the issue of combating moral hazard in finance by making firms liable for risky investment strategies, impact fees serve as a sort of insurance policy for local governments by pressuring firms to provide additional funding for projects. This in turn should push firms to carefully offer only their most profitable and socially practical proposals to permit committees.

Burge and Ihlanfeldt (2006) prove their theory with the data they found, yet there remains room for further research within the paper. The scope of their study is limited to just Florida and using their study to justify impact fees across national markets could prove problematic. While Florida is one of the top states in terms of the housing market, it does not fairly represent the average state's housing market. Additional research is needed to quantify a more definite understanding of the benefits of impact fees under more diverse circumstances. If it is the case that the Burge and Ihlanfeldt (2006) study is specific to Florida, the random trend and lagged dependent variables will become increasingly important in their findings. Further research could be conducted in order to back up their findings. While they did prove that impact fees do increase construction, one may wonder whether their results hold true in states other than Florida.

Multiple Choice Questions

1. According to Burge and Ihlanfeldt (2006) what was the total number of all types of houses that were increased due to nonwater/sewer impact fees in both inner and outer suburbs in the state of Florida?
   a. 1580
   b. 1820
   c. **1863**
   d. 1945

Explanation: Nonwater/sewer impact fees increased the number of new houses constructed by 1863 in Florida. There was an increase of 1393 in inner suburbs and 470 in outer suburbs. This was a 44-percent increase in inner suburbs and a 29-percent increase in outer suburbs. This increase represents a significant change due to nonwater/sewer impact fees for small-, medium-, and large-sized houses in both the inner and outer suburbs. Because of these impact fees the supply of houses increased significantly in Florida.

2. According to Burge and Ihlanfeldt (2006), which of the following is not an example of a provision of public services that benefit from impact fees?
   a. Water and Sewer
   b. Schools
   c. Roads
   d. **Hotels**

Explanation: Impact fees are involved in all of the above except for hotels. Water and sewer infrastructure is included in impact fees; however, for the sake of data in the paper, water and sewer are separated into their own type of impact fees. Schools and roads are a type of service that is a benefit to the community after completion so that they are affected by impact fees. Hotels are private construction that serves a benefit to a private market and not the local community, so the local government does not contribute to their construction.

3. According to Burge and Ihlanfeldt (2006), what is the best description of an impact fee?
   a. **Impact fees are one-time levies, predetermined through a formula adopted by a local government unit, that are assessed on property developers during the permit approval process**

b. Impact fees are multiple time levies, predetermined through a formula adopted by a local government unit, that are assessed on property developers during the permit approval process

c. Impact fees are one-time levies, predetermined through a formula adopted by a local government unit, that are assessed on property developers during the construction process

d. Impact fees are multiple time levies, predetermined through a formula adopted by a local government unit, that are assessed on property developers during the construction process

Explanation: Impact fees are predetermined by the local government through a formula that specific government adopted. They are only one-time levies and assessed on the developers during the permit approval process. They were created to be used for building public infrastructure services such as roads, schools, parks, and other recreational areas, libraries, and water and sewer. They are not multiple time levies and they do not take place during the construction period.

References

Burge, G. and K. Ihlanfeldt (2006), "Impact Fees and Single-Family Home Construction," Journal of Urban Economics 60, 284–306.

Mian, A. and A. Sufi (2014), "House of Debt," The University of Chicago Press: Chicago, USA.

CHAPTER 10

Property Taxation

In collaboration with Dane Lindholm and Malachi Rhoden

One policy resource that governments have is the power of taxation. Selectively making certain areas tax havens creates incentives for development to occur in these designated areas. They can stimulate spending and development; an important concept when analyzing how to meet certain urban-planning goals.

During a prior stage of inequality in the late 1800s, social reformer Henry George proposed a new solution to motivate economic development. He proposed to "abolish all taxation save that upon land values" (George 1879). Since the financial crisis of 2008, much of the world has had difficulty incentivizing landowners to invest and construct on undeveloped land. Government agencies, the same that influence tax rates, must now consider strategies in regards to motivating owners to build upon their land. George's proposal to cut taxes on developed land would motivate landowners to build on their properties as a source of increasing cash flows through said tax break, and would therefore penalize landowners who choose not to build on their land. A reduced or nullified tax on developed land would increase productivity and could spur economic growth within a municipality.

Although models for the relationship of property taxes and the supply of housing have been extensively theorized since Henry George's proposal, sufficient data of empirical evidence has been difficult to come by. Fortunately, in May of 2007 Teemu Lyyikäinen published an article using mathematical models to analyze the empirical results of a Finnish tax reform from 2001 until 2007. The reform allowed municipalities to create a variation in the tax rates for undeveloped residential land, and contained quality data to estimate the impact of property tax incentives on housing construction. The goal of this reform was to give Finnish municipalities a method of encouraging housing construction by implementing tax incentives once undeveloped land was zoned for housing. The purpose was to investigate how implementation of a three-rate tax system that taxed undeveloped land at a higher rate than developed land, specifically zoned land, commercial buildings, or permanent dwellings, impacted housing starts and housing density within the region's municipalities.

Lyyikäinen's (2009) article introduces the Finnish property tax system and continues with an explanation of the theoretical mathematical model and the empirical results of this model. Lyyikäinen uses the data from the ALTIKA database, which provides data on housing starts, annual population, annual supply of buildings, and housing prices from Q1 of 1998 to Q3 of 2006. The total number of Finnish municipalities that implemented a three-rate system during the 2001 to 2007 period was 118 out of 416. This data was reinforced with property tax rates supplied by the Association of Finnish Local and Regional Authorities (*Kuntaliitto*). The final property tax rates that the Finnish government implemented in 2007 after the results of the reform analyzed were: (1) a general property tax including land zoned and commercial buildings of 0.50 to 1.00 percent, (2) a property tax on permanent dwellings of 0.22 to 0.50 percent, and (3) a property tax on undeveloped residential land lots of 1.00 to 3.00 percent.

The theoretical model used was an alteration of Turnbull's (1988) model, as Turnbull's definition of "landowner value" contained only essential assumptions about urban rent prices from capital for construction. The model was further modified to represent the Finnish property tax system. This dynamic model calculates the present value of the parcel of land by adding the land rent in nonhousing use and the market rent based on the amount of capital used in construction. The model then subtracts off the effective building tax rate based on capital used in construction, the tax on land based on the raw site value, and the effective postdevelopment land tax. This calculation, however, is conditional on structural density and timing of development. Economically, it would be estimated that the theoretical observed effect of the property taxes on start time and density would depend on the incremental returns of a new housing investment.

The empirical model follows a count data analysis similar to the Plassmann and Tideman (2000) model that analyzed the two-rate property tax system. Lyyikäinen (2007) estimates the fixed-effects Poisson (FEP) model proposed by Hausman et al. (1984), who assumed that variance equals mean under weak assumptions is consistent with an estimated Beta parameters. Lyyikäinen specifically chose this model because it allowed for them to not specify a start time for development (no dependence between acquisition and development), in addition to accommodating the volume of buildings started. This is important economically since the theoretical model does not account for the number of buildings started, so the definition of "developed land" could be subjective. In such a case, landowners could potentially build anything to benefit from a lower tax rate. The final model used had two objectives: (1) to estimate the number of housing starts (timing of development) due to the effect of property taxes and (2) to estimate the volume (development density) of housing starts due to the effect of property taxes.

Due to the use of actual data on housing starts to measure construction activity, as well as a large sample size contributing to the estimates of interest, the quality of the Finnish data used in this study is high. When comparing the municipalities that maintained a two-rate tax system against municipalities that adopted a three-rate tax system at some point during 2001 to 2007, the results verify that a three-rate tax system promotes more single-family housing starts. This seemed particularly effective for any municipality that adopted the three-rate tax system in 2003 or 2004, while the evidence is less conclusive for the municipalities that adopted the three-rate tax in 2006 or 2007. One possible explanation of this discrepancy is that the three-rate tax system was implemented later in the year in 2006 and 2007, so the developers had less time to react to the new systems.

To further analyze the data, two FEP regressions were used to calculate the effect of both single-family housing starts and all housing starts on both a three-rate tax dummy variable and the control variables. The control variables used in the study included housing prices, housing stock per capita, province effects per year, and common quarter dummies. The first regression estimated the effect of property taxation with a dummy variable indicating the tax rate system of the municipality, while the second used a complete set of tax rates. The first regression will not suffer measurement errors in tax rates, but contained less detail than the regression with a complete set of tax rates.

The results of the first regression suggest that single-family homes are more susceptible for housing starts with a three-rate tax system than all housing starts. The coefficient of the three-rate tax system for single-family homes (0.121) is highly significant and suggests that the three-rate tax system increases single-family homes starts by 12.1 percent per unit of time. In contrast, the volume per start coefficient is insignificant to indicate that the density of development is not impacted by the three-rate tax system. The coefficient of the three-rate tax system on all housing starts is 8.7 percent, which is less than single-family housing starts, and the volume per building was –2.7 percent, which is again, statistically insignificant. Although the volume per building number is insignificant, the negative sign could hint that the three-rate taxation could lead to slightly lower densities. The reason that single-family housing starts may be more responsive to tax incentives could be that single-family homes are more impacted by land taxes than multi-unit housing.

The results of the regression with the complete set of tax rates follows a similar trend to the tax system dummy regression, by demonstrating a significant increase in housing starts due to the new tax rates, but not giving sufficient evidence of an increase in housing density. One benefit of the large variety within the sample size for this regression is that there is significant variation in the differences of tax rates over time within municipalities. Thus, the result of this regression parallels the theoretical model by indicating that higher taxes on undeveloped land incentivize development.

The overall empirical results of the Finnish data suggest that higher taxation on undeveloped land, as compared to developed land, has a positive effect on single-family housing starts, but not on the density or volume of the development. While all-housing starts seem to also be affected by the higher taxation on undeveloped land, the results seem to be less responsive than only single-family starts in the Finnish taxation example. A further conclusion is that development decisions do not impact the base land tax. This signifies that if municipalities have a uniform land tax rate, then development is not affected by land taxes.

The conclusions of this case illustrate how tax rates can stimulate spending within an economy. This relates to Mian and Sufi's (2014) novel, "House of Debt", as it confirms consistent evidence that spending or consumption can stimulate an economy that is hurting, or in a recession. For instance, the conclusions from the Finnish three-rate taxation test show that higher land taxes could incentivize landowners to develop on their land to avoid these increased costs. This, in turn, would create more jobs in the construction sector and promote increased consumption within an economy. The increased spending within an economy could bring said economy out of a recession, and shows how governments, or municipalities can play an essential role in revitalizing an economy.

While the results of Lyyikäinen's (2009) paper help to provide empirical evidence on a theoretical idea that has existed since the late nineteenth century, there are an identified few weaknesses in the paper's results. First, the results of the Finnish example are from a single period in time (2001 to 2007). Therefore, the reactions to increased development could reflect the market conditions for the time the study occurred, instead of from the taxation reform. This could be the reason why the implementation of the three-rate system in 2003 and 2004 had much stronger results than the implementation of the three-rate system in 2006 and 2007. A second weakness of the paper is that Lyyikäinen used an assumed fixed tax rate difference between predevelopment tax rates and postdevelopment tax rates in the theoretical model. It would be interesting to repeat this study by testing different pre- and post-development tax rates with both larger and smaller differentials. To see if the results of the study remain consistent and could be imposed as a tax incentive globally, one could replicate this research in an economy indicating signs that it is headed toward or already in a recession. If taxing undeveloped land at a higher rate has a correlation to increased spending due to construction and other areas of developmental spending, then it could potentially help to bring economies out of a possible recession.

Multiple Choice Questions

1. Ideally, according to Lyyikäinen (2009), what would be the expected outcome of imposing a three-rate tax system on undeveloped land versus a two-rate tax system?
   a. Landowners would cease building on the land in order to decrease the amount since building tax rates are highest
   b. **Landowners would have an incentive to build on the land since undeveloped residential lots would have the highest tax rate**
   c. Landowners would cease to build houses since they are heavily taxed
   d. Land owners would have an incentive to build commercial buildings since they have the lowest tax rate

Explanation: The correct answer is (b): The lowest tax rate would be on residential properties (permanent dwellings) at a rate of 0.22 to 0.5 percent which would rule out (b) and (d). The middle tax rate would be on zoned land and commercial buildings at a rate of 0.5 to 1 percent, making (a) false. Option (b) is the only option left and is correct since undeveloped residential lots would have the highest tax of 1 to 3 percent%, so landowners should have an incentive to build on that land.

2. According to Lyyikäinen (2009), what would be the long-term effect of the adoption of a higher property tax rate on undeveloped land?
   a. **The effect of adopting a higher tax on undeveloped land should start to decrease over time**
   b. The effect of adopting a higher tax on undeveloped land should start to increase over time
   c. There would be no change on the effect since the availability of land would remain stable

Explanation: The correct answer is (a): Higher taxes on undeveloped land would serve as an incentive to develop on land. This would cause landowners to develop on their land immediately to benefit from the tax incentive. As a result, there would be faster development on land and, overtime, there would be less land to develop on so the overall effect would start to decline. According to the scholarly research, the effects of the tax incentives start to weaken due to approaching toward an equilibrium.

3. According to Lyyikäinen (2009), increasing tax on undeveloped land had the greatest positive effect on which of the following type(s) of real estate properties?

   a. Zoned land and commercial building

   b. Single-family housing units

   c. Multi-family housing units

   d. All housing units

   e. (a) and (b)

Explanation: The correct answer is (b): Based on the data presented by Lyyikäinen (2009), 444 of single housing family houses that were started were due to tax incentives created by the three-rate tax system. This was a 3-percent increase in total single-family housing units started in 2005. When analyzing the tax system dummy regression in the article, the single-family homes had a 12.1-percent increase in housing starts, while all housing starts had only an 8.7-percent increase. Similarly, in the Poisson tax rates regression, the single-family homes had a 5.5-percent increase in development starts compared to 4.6-percent increase in starts for all housing. Therefore, single-family housing starts were concluded to be the greatest observable increase due to the implementation of a three-rate tax system.

References

George, H. (1879), "Progress and Poverty: An Inquiry into the Cause of Industrial Depressions and of Increase of Want with Increase of Wealth; The Remedy," Modern Library: New York.

Hausman, J., B. H. Hall and Z. Griliches (1984), "Econometric Models for Count Data with an Application to the Patents — R & D Relationship," Econometrica 52, 909–938.

Lyytikäinen, T. (2009), "Three-rate property taxation and housing construction," Journal of Urban Economics 65, 305–313.

Mian, A. and A. Sufi (2014), "House of Debt," University of Chicago Press: Chicago, USA.

Plassmann, F. and T. N. Tideman (2000), "A Markov Chain Monte Carlo Analysis of the Effect of Two-Rate Property Taxes on Construction," Journal of Urban Economics 47, 216–247.

Turnbull, G. K. (1988), "Property Taxes and the Transition of Land to Urban Use," Journal of Real Estate Finance and Economics 1, 393–403.

CHAPTER 11

Two-Rate Property Taxes on Construction

In collaboration with Tyler Piddington and Maxx Marcus

Taxes have, for a long while, been a hotly contested subject in the United States and all over the rest of the world. The premise is simple, take some money from everyone in a society and use it to provide services that are better provided by the government than by private enterprise. A good idea on the face, but how exactly should it operate? Who should pay what amount? What is this amount based on: income, wealth, the value of property owned? What should these funds support: poverty relief, housing inadequacies, infrastructure, health care, public safety? Politicians and the general public constantly debate these questions. Some argue in favor of a progressive tax, that the wealthy should pay more as they possess more and it is less of a burden on them. Others argue a flat tax is fairer; everyone pays their "fair share" of the burden. The uses of the proceeds of these tax dollars is an equally debated topic, but one that usual centers around personal beliefs.

The main goal of Plassman and Tideman (2011) is to evaluate the effectiveness and impact of a two-rate property tax system, particularly in light of what happens to construction activity. A two-rate tax system is one where land is taxed at a higher rate than improvements. In all 50 states, except Pennsylvania, land and improvements are taxed at the same rate. The hypothesis put forth by Plassman and Tideman, is that if a two-rate system was implemented, construction activity would increase. Within this overarching goal, the authors also examine and analyze previous studies which did not show a statistically significant impact of the two-rate taxes in Pennsylvania in an attempt to determine why they reached the conclusions they did and to find ways to appropriately adjust the data to achieve a statistically significant result.

In a general sense, Plassman and Tideman (2010) use construction data from Pennsylvania to show that cities that have adopted a two-rate tax experience higher level of construction activity than they would if they had a one-rate tax in place. What makes the specific data used in this study so critical is that there are peculiarities in the data that make the distributional assumptions used of great importance. The reason for this is that there are years where municipalities don't experience any new construction, so this places a large value at zero, which skews the distribution. In terms of which construction permits are useful to the study, the Bureau of the Census has created 21 different categories of building permits. Of those categories, 18 refer to new construction, while 3 consist of additions and alterations to existing buildings (not new construction of whole units). For the purpose of the study, the authors omitted permits from these three categories. The authors then ran a number of tests based on population trends to eliminate municipalities that were significantly different. After this, the authors had 219 municipalities, of which 15 had adopted a two-rate tax.

The main goal of the paper is to determine whether or not a two-rate tax has any effect of the rate of new construction. This appears to be a complicated question to answer and one that is far from straightforward to answer. After careful consideration, Plassman and Tideman (2010) address the distributional problem by first analyzing the effect of two-rate taxes on the number of building permits, and then their effect on the value per permit; the product of the two estimates yields an estimate of the effect of two-rate taxes on the total value of construction. In order to do this kind of analysis, the authors needed to separate the tax impact on the number of building permits and on the value per permit for four different categories of construction (residential whole units, residential additions and alterations, nonresidential whole units, and nonresidential additions and alterations). As far as economic intuition, their method makes sense in terms of finding the value of construction through the number of permits multiplied by the value of the permits and making a comparison across one-rate and two-rate municipalities. A large part of Plassman and Tideman's contribution to this topic is their use of a Poisson distribution instead of the standard distributions used by previous academics. The Poisson distribution is positively skewed and so it is much better suited for the type of data (significant number of zeros) that this research yielded. The Poisson distribution gave their results much more statistical significance than previous studies that used standard regression models.

The authors found that previous analyses of the impact of two-rate taxes used standard regression techniques and focused on the value of construction. The standard regression models did not fit the data well, thus many previous findings were not statistically significant. What makes Plassman and Tiderman's research different is that they examined separately the tax impact on the number of building permits and on the value per permit. By separating out the tax effect on number and value of permits and by using a Poisson distribution, they were able to find a positive and statistically significant impact on the number of permits. The estimated overall impact on the total value of construction is positive and statistically significant.

In conclusion, there is a statistically significant positive impact on construction activity when a two-rate tax is imposed. This is logical because if the value of improvements is taxed at a lower rate than land, there is incentive to develop the land into something more economically productive. In the case where land and buildings are taxed at the same rate, construction is discouraged as it increases the tax burden on the property owner relative to the two-rate system. There is evidence that it does increase construction; some would argue this is good for society, whereas others would argue the opposite. A lower rate on improvements also raises the question of where that shortfall in tax revenue would come from; which of course lends itself to a multitude of options, none of which everyone would agree on. While Plassman and Tideman conclude a two-rate tax leads to more construction, the best use of this information is another question.

If the authors were to do further research on this topic, it would be interesting to see what the effects of the two-rate tax are in other areas besides construction activity. For example, are other tax rates higher to make up for the shortfall from taxing structures at a lower rate? Are cities with two-rates even able to make up for the shortfall or do they experience frequent budget deficits? Additional research could also consist of surveys to developers and other players in the market to see how they view the two different taxing systems and any effects the difference has in the eyes of a developer. Additional research could also include looking internationally at what other countries do when it comes to taxing real estate. Do they even tax it? Do they use a one- or two-rate system? The answers to these questions would provide valuable insight into the desirability of a two-rate system. Perhaps more states/municipalities will adopt this system in the future if it is believed that the benefits it provides by stimulating construction offset the revenues lost from a lower rate on structures.

Multiple Choice Questions

1. According to Plassman and Tideman (2010), what was the impact of the two-rate tax system based on the total value of construction?
   a. **The estimated overall impact on the total value of construction is positive and statistically significant**
   b. The estimated overall impact on the total value of construction is positive and statistically insignificant
   c. The estimated overall impact on the total value of construction is negative and statistically insignificant
   d. The estimated overall impact on the total value of construction is negative and statistically significant

Explanation: Based on the findings of Plassman and Tideman's study the impact of the two-rate tax system based on the total value of construction is positive and statistically significant. Also the impact was found to be positive and statistically significant based on the number of permits, but statistically insignificant for the value per individual permit.

2. According to the Building Categories in the Bureau of the Census Data Set, which of the following selections are actual building permit categories?
   a. **Single-family houses**
   b. **Addition of garages and carports**
   c. **Three-and four-family buildings**
   d. **Industrial buildings**
   e. Barns

Explanation: After reviewing Plassman and Tideman (2010); results and viewing the building categories, one can clearly pick out answers (a)–(d) and see that they are all actual building permit categories of both the residential housekeeping buildings as well as the residential nonhouse-keeping buildings and nonresidential buildings. Answer (e) was incorrect as a barn is not its own category but would fall under a nonresidential structure other than a building.

3. What assumption is made under the Poisson model and why is this essential to the study of Plassman and Tideman (2010)?

   a. The data have a variance that is equal to their mean; it's essential to this study because the distribution is meant to model the number of building permits issued, a number that can't be negative and will be positively skewed as it is typical for only a small number of permits to be issued in a given municipality in a given year

   b. The data have a variance that is greater than their mean; it's essential to this study because the distribution is meant to model the number of building permits issued, a number that varies greatly and will often be positively skewed as the number of permits issued in a given municipality in a given year is highly unpredictable

   c. The data have a variance that is less than their mean; it's essential to this study because the distribution is meant to model the number of building permits issued, a number that doesn't vary in a given municipality in a given year

   d. There are no assumptions when using the Poisson Model

Explanation: In this study the answer is (a), based on the findings of both Plassman and Tideman (2010) and the needed use of the Poisson Model. It is essential to the study because it is meant to model the number of building permits issued. In addition, we do not believe that the observed request for buildings is best conveyed as a distinct outcome of an otherwise unceasing choice process, but that the Poisson process defines the demand for such structures more accurately.

References

Plassman, F. and T. N. Tideman (2010), "A Markov Chain Monte Carlo Analysis of the Effect of Two-Rate Property Taxes on Construction," Journal of Urban Economics 47, 216–247.

Plassmann, F. and T. N. Tideman (2011), "Marginal Cost Pricing and Eminent Domain," Foundations and Trends in Microeconomics 7, No. 1 1–110.

PART V

Housing Supply

CHAPTER 12

Construction Cycles

In collaboration with Will Metzfield and Charles Nulsen

The cycle that construction levels go through can be used as a key economic indicator that reflects the general state of the economy. Understanding construction cycles allows for the understanding of why the markets are behaving the way they are, as well as giving a sort of predictive base for future events to be based off.

The Federal Reserve made a controversial decision to continue not to raise rates as they didn't believe the economy had climbed back enough from the collapse in 2007 yet. With a current interest rate near zero, the economy should be stimulated enough to grow at a steady pace, yet this doesn't seem to be the case. Caterpillar, a large industrial supplier recently reported its lowest growth in years, citing issues with oil prices and decreased construction demand. Internationally the economy is in a similar situation with a general distrust of world powers including China who has recently come under fire for their internal stock market rigging. The international and domestic economic landscape haven't been in a situation like this as growth is starting to stagnate without a promising momentous event to push it forward.

Leland Burns and Leo Grebler have investigated the instability of total construction and its major sectors. The authors believe this study was necessary due to the lack of attention this issue has received. According to the report, the last comprehensive study of construction cycles took place in 1982. This is surprising because construction is a large sector of the economy, meaning a lack of knowledge on this topic could lead to an inefficient use of human and material capital. Grebler and Burns' goal is to use empirical data to construct theories on the relationships between cycles of total construction and its components and between construction and gross national product (GNP) cycles. Their main concern with this research is to answer whether the components of the construction cycle have become more or less volatile over time, and if public policy has any effect on these cycles. Even with extensive research on this topic, Grebler and Burns admit that the unique heterogeneity of this industry results in very complicated relationships and limits the accuracy of cyclical analysis.

The data used for the study came from the national income accounts and represent quarterly expenditures at adjusted annual rates in 1972 dollars. The study breaks down the construction into four sectors: private residential, private nonresidential, public federal, and public state and local construction. The author's qualifications of each construction are dictated by the ownership criterion used in the official data. Thus, private residential buildings can include construction activity aided by a large variety of government programs. The only residential buildings assigned to the public sector are projects that were formerly classified as "public housing." Likewise in the public sector, buildings assigned to state and local construction can include projects that were partially funded by federal grants or loans. Only direct federal constructions appear under the designation of public federal construction.

The cycles studied in construction are delineated from trends in GNP and business fixed investments (BFIs), which serve as "reference cycles." This trend adjustment makes it possible to pinpoint the cyclical fluctuations more precisely. In order to distinguish movements in construction expenditures from cycle phases and erratic changes, the authors require a cyclical trend to have at least three calendar quarters of consistent upward or downward movement.

The economic impact of these cyclical changes is widespread. Market contractions conclude in a large decrease in usage of resources required for building as well as a dispersal of labor for the market, with an unlikely probability of return. Market expansions require large amounts of labor to flow into the system, as well as advanced training for new entrants into the workforce. The overall market implications have been proven important enough to begin public works projects by the federal and state governments for years now. As an overarching concept, construction encompasses modest remodel work in existing spaces, to multimillion dollar skyscraper building in Manhattan, NYC.

Burns and Grebler (1982) main findings can be broken down into three distinct categories: number, duration, and amplitude of the cycles. The number of cycles seems to be the first point of differentiation between the analyzed data—private and public construction cycles as well as their sector differentials—and the proposed reference cycles—GNP and BFI. The analyzed data has gone through a total of 29 cycles when aggregated, while the reference data has had 4 total cycles. The number of construction cycles showed that individual sectors of the economy can move without matching movements in total output.

As for duration, the cycles haven't shown a great deal of change over time, with few trends being drawn in each cycle. The main duration trend found was the lengthening of the average private construction cycle, and the shortening of the nonresidential cycles since the 1960s. The last measure, amplitude, proved to be the biggest source of findings in the research itself. With amplitude came the measurement of volatility within total construction and the private-sector counterparts. This volatility has increased since the 1950s across all sectors, as cyclical swings have had amplitudes greater than the previous cycles. The only exception to the increased volatility was Federal construction which showed diminished volatility. With construction's cyclical fluctuations coming under much review recently, economists have begun taking additional looks at all sectors, rather than just the housing cycle like they had previously.

The main conclusion from the article would have to be the increase in volatility within private construction, along with its residential counterpart and total construction. What surprised the researchers was the fact that the government had added governmental housing policies and public works programs in an attempt to stabilize the residential sector; however, the volatility had increased showing higher amplitudes within the fluctuations. In addition, research on older construction cycles (between 1950 and 1978) yielded intriguing results when taking a look at the timing and average amplitude of the construction cycles. As a whole, the total construction sector has been the largest source of volatility within the aggregated market. In connection with the residential building sector, the belief that output of new housing was counteracted by instability was proven false as public and private construction moved in opposite directions. As a generalized note on the cyclical nature of the findings, public construction has long been procyclical, while private has leaned countercyclical.

As for the macroeconomic variable GNP and its congruence with these construction cycle fluctuations, they found that aggregate construction tended to match up with the same reference peaks and troughs of the total output reference numbers, although this wasn't always a catch all for the research. In additional, residential construction seemed to predict changes in GNP, by consistently leading turning points in GNP, with the mean upswing turning a year before GNP expansion had stopped. The biggest conclusion in Burns and Grebler is that their results are consistent with the hypothesis that changes in financial conditions, sometimes supplemented by actions of the federal housing credit agencies, are prime determinants of the residential cycle. In general, the findings of the paper showcase the relationships found between the cycles of total construction and its association with the major construction sectors, along with its connections with fluctuations found in total output. The summation leads to the macroreason that this research would be useful, and why it was necessary in the first place. This macroreason was something that was derived from the markets as a whole, that being why the government, more specifically policy makers, are continuously search for ways of using public construction investment as a mean for mediating economic instability in the aggregated marketplace.

As mentioned in the Mian and Sufi's book "House of Debt", during the Great Recession the effects of debt expanded far beyond the indebted. When the housing market collapsed, problems were created for the entire economy beyond the banking sector. This spillover effect included higher unemployment and a failing construction sector. Contractions in the construction sector resulted many externalities including underutilized resources and a dispersal of construction labor. The market for construction labor is extremely unique and hard to stimulate because construction projects are limited in length and the workplace location is constantly shifting. These qualities make construction labor fairly unattractive, which results in difficult expansion of this labor market. Therefore, it is not astonishing that expanded public works programs are used to counteract declines in construction.

As far as weaknesses of Burns and Grebler (1982) go, we will run through a few below, but to clarify, these are not due to common writing issues including bias and misinformation, but rather the lack of updated information and prior research on the topic. In conjunction with this lack of updated information, there was a lack of connection between the research conducted and the modern market decision making, ultimately making the data less applicable to current scenarios.

Reading this in the current day makes this piece seem like the new reference point that one might use to reanalyze the current cycles. This paper also lacks specific depth within the individual markets; however, this data may not have been available at the time of research. Overall the weaknesses of the paper are few and far between, but all in all it can be improved upon through additional research and in-depth analysis of current trends.

After pointing out the above weaknesses, we have included some suggestions for future research in our summary. First, future research should be updated beyond 1982 as construction cycles are happening at a much faster pace due to the advancement of technology as well as increased methods of building. This research will then serve as the new reference material for this future-based research. In addition, researching more stratified sectors will allow for a deeper understanding of sector growth within the aggregate construction market. Understanding the construction differences between retail, office, multifamily, and so on, would allow for a greater depth of analysis across all cycles. The authors even pointed out areas of additional research that would benefit the piece including further research on the effectiveness of public construction and its effect on economic stability.

Multiple Choice Questions

1. According to Burns and Grebler (1982), the analysis of the amplitude of cyclical fluctuations reveals:
   a. Decreasing volatility of total construction and its major private-sector components
   b. **Increasing volatility of total construction and its major private-sector components**
   c. No change in volatility of total construction and its major public-sector components
   d. Increasing volatility of total construction and its major public-sector components

Explanation: This finding is extremely surprising because volatility increased despite the growth of federal credit programs, which are designed to moderate the adverse effects of "tight money" in housing. Therefore, the increase in volatility can be explained by either the changes of general financial conditions and monetary policy, which may have exceeded the influence of housing credit agencies, or by nonfinancial variables. According to the report, cyclical swings have become more severe in total construction since the 1950s and in private construction since the 1960s.

2. According to Burns and Grebler (1982), what were the prime determinants of the residential construction cycle?

   a. **Changes in financial conditions, supplemented by actions of the federal housing credit agencies**

   b. Changes in economic growth, fueled by increased lending by banks due to increased consumer demand

   c. Changes in financial conditions, disregarding the actions made by the federal housing credit agencies

   d. Changes in construction cycles due to decrease in consumer housing demand

Explanation: One of the main functioning hypothesis utilized throughout the piece was the quote: "The results are consistent with the hypothesis that changes in financial conditions, sometimes supplemented by actions of the federal housing credit agencies, are prime determinants of the residential cycle." It is important for readers to understand the drives behind the cycles because without understanding what moves the cycle, you can't truly understand how they interact. A movement in one cycle generally has some correlation to a movement in another cycle, may it be countercyclical or procyclical.

3. According to Burns and Grebler (1982), which of the following statements is true?

   a. Residential construction is not highly dependent on external financing or high sensitivity to cost

   b. In business recessions, the financial determinates do not change with the construction field entering into a contractionary phase

   c. Economic expansion is attributed to an increase in demand from business for borrowed funds and simultaneous increase of interest rates

   d. Cyclical movements in housing tend to run in congruence with those of GNP

Explanation: All of these options come from the "Countercyclical" portion of the paper. They are all related when it pertains to the residential building movements and what ebbs and flows within the cycles themselves. Option (c) is the correct choice as expansion is often attributed to increased demand for money as well as a lower bound interest rate. Option (a) is not correct due to the word NOT; the statement would be true had that not been there. Option (b) is not correct as the financial determinates reverse in this situation, leading to an expansionary phase, not a contractionary one. Finally, option (d) is incorrect as housing tends to fun opposite of the movements in GNP.

References

Burns, L. and L. Grebler (1982), "Construction Cycles in the United States Since World War II," Real Estate Economics 10, 123–151.

Mian, A. and A. Sufi (2014), "House of Debt," University of Chicago Press: Chicago, USA.

CHAPTER 13

Reinvestment in the Housing Stock

In collaboration with Steven Quinn and Tian Zhan

Imagine holding a steady, quality manufacturing job for many years in one of America's many traditional industrial cities such as Detroit, Buffalo, or Cleveland. You are raising a family in a modest urban home in this city when suddenly the job you have depended on for your whole career no longer exists. And you are not alone in this situation as thousands of other workers are facing the same difficult circumstances. Faced with limited job prospects staying in the city or the possibility that exists outside of it, many families choose to relocate in hopes of finding work. This shift in the population of many urban cities has served as a strong negative shock to demand for housing within these cities resulting in plummeting home values. Much research in public policy has focused on addressing this issue of falling home values related to the demand shock from relocating families. But what about the families who choose to stay? Will these families choose to reinvest in their homes through remodeling and renovations even in the face of falling home value? Gyourko and Saiz (2004) argue that the supply side of the housing market, specifically the relationship between home value and construction costs, also has an impact on the outcome of a negative demand shock to urban housing markets.

The purpose of this research is to understand whether the negative demand shock in many urban housing markets caused by relocation of families away from these manufacturing-focused cities is the only driver of the decline in these urban housing markets or whether the supply side of the housing market also contributes to the overall impact on declining cities. In order to make this determination, the Gyourko and Saiz (2004) use the data sources described below to see whether homeowners reinvest in their homes less often when the construction cost in their market exceeds the market value of the home. The overall goal from this research is to encourage policy makers to consider the impact construction costs have on the urban decline of these cities in addition to the current focus on addressing the demand side issues of the urban housing markets.

Gyourko and Saiz (2004) utilized three main sources to get the necessary information for their research. For the house price and renovation expenditure data, they relied on the American Housing Survey (AHS). The housing data used from this survey as part of the research included data collected between 1984 and 1994 for various urban housing markets in the United States. The RS Means Company is used as the source for information related to construction costs. This data again provides information on urban housing markets throughout the United States as well as certain urban housing markets in Canada. In order to compare prices and costs across time periods, the Urban Consumer Price Index (CPI-U) is used to convert all dollar amounts to 2001 dollar values.

In order to find the relationship between construction costs, home values, and home reinvestment expenditures, Gyourko and Saiz build a simple regression model. The data is based on the data from the above sources for 43 urban housing markets.

Gyourko and Saiz (2004) propose a Tobit model with an uncensored latent variable for renovation expenditures as the dependent variable. The independent variables are a metropolitan statistical area (MSA) fixed effect, a year fixed effect, a dummy that takes a value of one if the unit is valued below construction cost, home value, and a vector of household variables including home age, number of rooms, household income, unit square footage, and a dummy for the presence of a porch. They expect this combination of independent variables to influence household renovation expenditures and try to determine the coefficient of each independent variable. After analyzing the data, it was found that each of these coefficients is positive. This means that each of these variables such as home value and household variables such as home age, number of rooms have a positive relationship with household renovation spending. An increase in any of these factors tends to increase household renovation spending while a decrease would result in less spending. For example, the data show that a sharp fall in house prices will decrease renovation spending. Through this experiment and data, Gyourko and Saiz (2004) point out a significant negative impact of $240 less in renovation spending if the home value is below construction cost.

However, the result is robust and may be imprecise. Gyourko and Saiz (2004) explain how endogeneity and measurement error may influence the experiment result. Endogeneity, to be discussed in more detail later, is related to whether the model can point toward a specific cause of the correlations that the model finds. Measurement error can be caused by the data used in the model. These two factors are potential areas of bias in the initial regression model. In order to make an unbiased and more precise model for the relationship between renovation spending, home prices, and construction costs, Gyourko and Saiz propose a second equation using a modified dummy variable to replace the initial dummy variable used in the first equation. This new dummy variable still relates home values to construction costs, but does so in a slightly different way to reduce the measurement bias. The new dummy variable will take a value of one if the *average* home value of all other units in the specific tract is below construction cost and zero otherwise. This equation provides a new ratio relating house prices to construction cost (P/CC). If P/CC is larger than one, it means the home values are greater than construction costs and the dummy variable will be equal to one. This equation is very important not only for its further explanation of the original equation, but also for decreasing the error and bias in the initial regression model by creating a more accurate two least square model.

Adding this new equation to the model further strengthens the results and makes the relationship between home values, construction cost, and renovation spending even more clear. Before, there was a $240 decrease in renovation spending if house value was less than construction cost, but after, this number rises to $911 in the modified regression model. To be clear, this means that households on average spend $911 less in household renovation when the home value is below construction cost.

The result is nonsurprising and pretty straightforward. If a house is valued under its construction cost, people will invest less in home renovations which demonstrates that an impact is indeed caused by the supply side of declining housing markets in addition to the decline caused by a negative demand shock. Homeowners want to invest in their house when there is a positive rate of return. But when construction cost exceeds the benefit, few homeowners will make the decision to reinvest in additional spending on their home resulting in further deterioration of urban housing markets in which construction costs exceed home values.

An immense amount of additional research has been done in relation to declining housing markets. One example of this is the book "House of Debt" by Atif Mian and Amir Sufi. This book is similar to Gyourko and Saiz (2004) in that their research also looks into the implications of declining home prices. However, the focus for Mian and Sufi (2014) is the role that debt plays in the decline of an economy when faced with falling home values. This is in contrast to the article which focuses on the role of construction costs in relation to falling home prices. However, in their analysis of the subprime mortgage crisis, Mian and Sufi do briefly use the same reasoning that Gyourko and Saiz use regarding the relationship that construction costs and home prices have on spending. Gyourko and Saiz (2004) argue that homeowners tend to reinvest in their home with additional spending much more often when the value of their home exceeds construction costs. However, their findings suggest that homeowners do so much less once the price of their home falls below the cost of construction. In making their argument that increased mortgage debt caused the housing bubble, rather than the other way around, Mian and Sufi use a similar line of thinking but in the context of housing-supply elasticity. Mian and Sufi state that, "If housing prices rise above construction costs, supply responds quickly by building more houses" in regards to elastic housing supply cities with land available for construction. While this focuses on new construction rather than reinvestment expenditures, the same theory, that spending decreases when construction cost exceeds home values, is used by both Gyourko and Saiz (2004) and Mian and Sufi (2014). Based on both studies, the support for the relationship between home value, construction cost, and spending seems very strong.

Although the data collected and conclusions drawn by Gyourko and Saiz (2004) based on their research is very convincing and meaningful, there are a couple areas of weakness to consider in this paper. The main weakness is the issue of "endogeneity." What this issue really comes down to is the direction of the findings that renovation expenditures significantly decrease when house prices fall below construction costs. Specifically, do homeowners choose to stop investing in their homes because the value has fallen below construction cost or do home prices fall below construction cost because homeowners have stopped reinvesting in their home? The evidence and research certainly makes clear that a correlation exists between the ratio of home value to construction cost and its relationship with renovation expenditures. However, applying the evidence to support the direction of causation is more difficult. Gyourko and Saiz (2004) do indeed apply procedures to control for and support the conclusion that the drop in home values below construction cost causes reduced reinvestment; however, further research and support to prove this causation may be necessary. Another area that could make this research and findings stronger would be by proposing potential strategies to address the supply-side issue that the findings establish. Whether it is proposing specific public policy initiatives that could improve the problem or proposing additional research required to address the issue, a more specific discussion of the implications of the research findings could certainly strengthen the paper.

On that note, there are a few areas related to these findings that could benefit from further research in the future. One such area for future research would be identifying the driver behind construction cost for any given urban market. Gyourko and Saiz (2004) note that, "there is considerable variation in construction costs across metropolitan areas, and many declining areas are relatively costly." Research into this phenomenon would be useful when developing supply-side policies needed to lower construction cost and encourage home reinvestment despite falling home prices. If the findings are accurate and the market for construction projects is competitive, we would expect to see that declining areas with little demand for renovation construction work also have relatively cheap construction costs. However, the Gyourko and Saiz (2004) clearly state that this is not the case. As such, further research into an explanation for the underlying cause of this phenomenon is necessary in order to effectively address it. In addition to researching what drives construction costs in urban markets, future research around potential supply-side policies is needed in order to feasibly implement such policies. A look at if these types of policies have been implemented in certain markets, and the impact on that market, could be a good starting point for this research. Overall, the Gyourko and Saiz (2004) provide a very comprehensive look into the impact the relationship between house prices and construction costs has on home reinvestment. However, in order to make the most of these findings and apply them to address the issue of urban decline, future research is still necessary.

Multiple Choice Questions

1. According to the Gyourko and Saiz (2004), if the ratio of house price to construction cost (P/CC) is less than 1, should you expect the homeowner to reinvest in their home through various renovation projects?
   a. Yes
   b. **No**

Explanation: In order to determine the connection between home values, construction costs, and reinvestment expenditures, the Gyourko and Saiz (2004) utilize a regression model that includes a dummy variable for the ratio of home values divided by construction costs. The results show that if this ratio is greater than one, homeowners on average invest more often and with more money in their homes. On the other hand, as is asked in this question, if the ratio is less than one, homeowners consistently choose to reduce or eliminate renovation spending.

2. Gyourko and Saiz (2004) use two different equations as part of their regression model for their research. What role does the second equation play in the regression model?
   a. The second equation is used to answer a new research question based on the findings from the first equation
   b. **The second equation is a two-stage-square method which decreases the standard error of the first equation and makes the model more precise**
   c. The second equation was used for fun
   d. The second equation is used to collect additional data and reach a different conclusion

Explanation: The purpose of the second equation is to reduce the issue of endogeneity as well as to decrease the standard error present in the initial regression model. Without these two influencing factors of bias, the research findings become more precise. Not only do the coefficients of the independent variables become more significant, but also the reduction in renovation spending becomes even more pronounced in the second regression equation. The decrease in household spending on average went from $239 with the first equation to $911 in the second equation for houses valued below construction costs.

3. According to the Gyourko and Saiz (2004), which of the following is a main conclusion or implication reached based on this research?

   a. The supply-side of housing markets such as construction costs has no impact on the extent or degree of decline in urban housing markets

   b. If construction costs in a housing market exceed the value of a home, homeowners would likely choose to reinvest in their home through renovation expenditures

   c. **If construction costs in a housing market are less than the value of a home, homeowners are more likely to reinvest in their home through renovation expenditures**

   d. A conclusion could not be reached regarding the relationship between house prices, construction costs, and renovation expenditures

Explanation: (a) is incorrect because the purpose of the research is to find out if decline in urban housing markets is exclusively demand driven. Gyourko and Saiz (2004) conclude that the supply-side, specifically construction costs relative to home value, impact the homeowner's decision to reinvest in their homes. The relationship found by this research is that if construction costs are less than the value of the home, then homeowners are more likely to reinvest in their home through renovation expenditures. This is why (c) is the correct answer and (b) is incorrect. (d) is incorrect because the Gyourko and Saiz (2004) are able to reach a conclusion regarding this relationship.

References

Gyouko, J. and A. Saiz (2004), "Reinvestment in the Housing Stock: the Role of Construction Costs and the Supply Side," Journal of Urban Economics 55, 238–256.

Mian, A. and A. Sufi (2014), "House of Debt," University of Chicago Press: Chicago, USA.

CHAPTER 14

Estimating the Housing Supply

In collaboration with Jack Hoy and Robert Perina

According to a report by Reuters, housing starts in the United States have soared as of July 2015; new residential construction is at one of its highest levels in the last 8 years. While this is could be a good sign for the economy, many may wonder why this is happening. Clearly, there are a variety of factors that go into an increase in housing starts, but what are the most important ones? Christopher Mayer and Tsuriel Somerville present and analyze a model that helps answer this question, which leads to valuable conclusions about the implications of this economic signal.

Mayer and Somerville (2000) explain new housing construction as a function of changes in house prices and costs. To develop their model, they review previous empirical studies of housing supply, which consider residential development like other types of investments. In this paper, however, they try to present a model that incorporates how land differs from typical investments because supply of land is inelastic.

In order to develop their model, Mayer and Somerville used several sources of data to come to their conclusions. They first looked at figures showing the differences between housing starts and price levels in the United States. The paper, however, suggests that using this data limits explaining house starts and price levels because of its inconsistency. Instead, Mayer and Somerville use data that shows the relationship between housing starts and the changes in housing prices.

Mayer and Somerville (2000) rely on the previous findings regarding the relationship between starts and house prices to find how they can create a model that most accurately represents new housing construction.

Specifically, they look at the two approaches used by existing empirical studies. The first approach concludes that the supply curve for the housing starts is perfectly elastic, while the second approach estimates housing starts as a function of the level of house prices and cost shifters. Mayer and Somerville specifically describe the models created by Topel and Rosen (1988) and DiPasquale and Wheaton (1994), but they conclude that these models do not capture the role land plays in a model for housing starts.

After developing a model that depicts housing supply with consideration to the land development process in a single city, Mayer and Somerville use data to apply their model to the nation. Specifically, they use the Freddie Mac repeat sales index to measure house price movements to allow their supply model to be applicable to the United States. The authors do note that there can be problems with using sales indexes; however, the Freddie Mac repeat sales index matches up well with the model.

The paper argues that as a city's population increases, so does the amount of land it occupies, which increases housing prices and stock. The city then needs a greater number of housing starts to fill its existing stock. Therefore, housing starts and prices will be higher after an increase in population.

Mayer and Somerville use the data to develop a model for supply of new housing that is consistent with the land development process, which previous empirical models failed to accomplish. A main point in its model is that Mayer and Somerville realize that there are delays in developing land from nonurban use to residential use, and these delays must be accounted for in predicting demand.

Their model for housing starts accounts for the lag in price and cost changes, which depends on "the length of time required to obtain developed land, acquire housing permits, and builders' expectations about changes in future house prices."

Mayer and Somerville (2000) also present a model that shows that housing starts are a function of changes in construction costs and prices. They argue that the size of a city is directly correlated to the price and cost of housing. In their equations, new housing construction can be explained and estimated by changes in house prices and construction costs. The model, however, is best used for a single city.

Mayer and Somerville used data from the Freddie Mac repeat sales index, which shows quarterly changes in house prices from 1975 to 1974. In order to use this data effectively and compare it to existing models, they converted the Freddie Mac index to house price levels in 1991. Based on that data, Mayer and Somerville concluded that prices do not fully adjust to market equilibrium in the short run.

After running the regression, Mayer and Somerville found that the most significant variable was changes in house prices; a $943 increase led to a quarterly increase in housing starts of 18,300 units. They also found that changes in interest rates were statistically significant. However, these interest rate changes were not quite as impactful as the housing price changes. For instance, in the regression they ran, a 1.3-percent increase in interest rates decreased new housing starts by about 12,000 units. Furthermore, the authors found that one variable, material prices, did not end up being significant. Finally, Mayer and Somerville note that the variable of median time-to-sale, which takes into account market conditions, was significant and does impact new housing starts. More specifically, it is negatively correlated with construction. For instance, if one increases the median time-to-sale variable by one standard deviation, housing starts decrease by 16,300 units. Based on its significance, the authors determine that nonprice variables can also impact housing starts.

Mayer and Somerville conclude that changes in house prices and construction costs (lagged and current) are significant factors in determining new housing starts. They use their model to estimate that when house prices increase by 10 percent, housing stock increases by 0.8 percent. It is important to note that the variables used are changes in the level of prices and costs, not simply the levels of them. This is one of the reasons their model does well when compared to other notable models.

Mayer and Somerville also conclude that it only takes about 1 year for stock to adjust to a shock in demand, which is completely different from DiPasquale and Wheaton's (1994) estimate of 35 years. Finally, they determined that although an increase in house prices leads to more new construction, this increase is only temporary, not permanent. Overall, Mayer and Somerville create a model to show what factors impact new construction of houses and analyze the impact of their findings.

This article can be easily related to a variety of other real estate literature; in particular, the discussion of development in the book "Real Estate Principles: A Value Approach" seemed to be relevant to the article. In this article, the authors, David Ling and Wayne Archer, discuss what it is like to be a developer, noting that the process can be very unpredictable and complicated. This reflects what the article implies: there are numerous factors that go into construction of new housing. The authors of the article did an excellent job of creating a model to help predict housing starts, but it is important to note that the unpredictability of development in general could make the actual number of housing starts significantly different from what the model predicts.

Furthermore, Ling and Archer's book also discusses various types of construction costs. This is relatable to the article, as changes in construction costs were found to be a significant factor in housing starts. Some of the costs listed in the text include soft costs such as inspections and insurance and hard costs such as permits/fees. It is important to know all of the costs that go into the one construction cost variable.

Although the paper presents a very sound model to predict the construction of new houses, there is some potential for improvement in future research. First of all, much of the empirical analysis that Mayer and Somerville do is based on national data. However, their model is for an individual city. This mismatch forces them to rely on two assumptions: "First, that an urban form framework is applicable to national data; second, that there is a single national housing market." By having to rely on these assumptions, it increases the likelihood that this model may fail when actually used in practice. In addition, individual cities are very different from one another, which means that the model may be ineffective in one city but effective in another. Finally, when testing their model against other notable models, they use a small sample size that could create skewed results.

In the future, there are also other multiple concepts that the authors could continue to research. For instance, their article deals with the housing supply in one market. As the authors note, they would like to apply the model to different markets. By studying the supply across markets, they could introduce new factors that would affect new construction, such as governmental regulations.

Another idea would be to study new construction for nonresidential buildings. This would allow the researchers to potentially find any similarities between the variables that impact the supply of commercial and residential buildings, which could provide valuable information for the real estate industry.

Multiple Choice Questions

1. Which of the following is not a reason presented by Mayer and Somerville (2000) for a lag in price and cost changes?
   a. Length of time required to obtain developed land
   b. Acquiring housing permits
   c. Builders' expectations about changes in future house prices
   d. **Zoning changes required for urban development**

Explanation: Mayer and Somerville (2000) incorporate a lag in price and cost changes due to the length of time required to obtain developed land, acquiring housing permits, and builders' expectations about changes in future prices. Mayer and Somerville do not mention zoning changes as a reason for a lag in price and cost changes. They do, however, incorporate a lag for the other reasons because these delays often occur in developing land from nonurban uses to residential units. If the delay was not included in the model, the timing of housing starts would inaccurately be represented.

2. According to Mayer and Somerville (2000), after an increase in population, housing starts and prices will _____?
   a. **Both increase**
   b. Housing starts will decrease but prices will decrease
   c. Housing starts will increase but prices will increase
   d. Both decrease

Explanation: Housing starts and prices will both increase with an increase in population. This holds true because as a city's population increase so does its amount of land it occupies, which increases housing prices and stock. The city then needs a greater number of housing starts to fill its existing stock. A city with a higher population will then have a higher construction costs and housing starts. Housing starts, however, will only increase as needed to adjust to the increase in population.

3. According to Mayer and Somerville (2000), changes in _____ have the strongest effect on housing starts?
   a. Construction costs
   b. **Housing prices**
   c. Interest rates
   d. High unemployment rates

Explanation: In the regression in the paper, Mayer and Somerville show that housing prices have the strongest effect on housing starts. A $943 increase (which equates to one standard deviation) in housing prices, or one standard deviation, increases starts by 53,800 units in a year. Although interest rates have an effect on housing starts, but it is not nearly as impactful as an increase in housing prices. For comparison, a 1.3-percent increase (one standard deviation) in interest rates leads to 12,000 unit decrease in housing starts. Clearly, it is not as impactful as changes in housing prices. Interest rates affect the housing market through the demand instead of the supply. Higher interest rates and housing costs would cause a drop-off in housing start because they are negatively correlated.

References

DiPasquale, D. and W. C. Wheaton (1994), "Housing Market Dynamics and the Future of Housing Prices," Journal of Urban Economics 35, 1–28.

Ling, D. C. and W. R. Archer (2013), "Real Estate Principles: A Value Approach," 4th ed. US: McGraw-Hill Education, 625–628.

Mayer, C. J. and C. T. Somerville (2000), "Residential Construction: Using the Urban Growth Model to Estimate Housing Supply," Journal of Urban Economics 48, 85–109.

Mutikani, L. (2015), "U.S. Housing Starts Approach Eight-Year High in July," US: Thomson Reuters.

Topel, R. and S. Rosen (1988), "Housing Investment in the United States," Journal of Political Economy 96, 718–740.

CHAPTER 15

Movements in Office-Commercial Construction

In collaboration with Mackalister Gapinski and Karim Nassef

The real estate industry is notorious for its booms and busts. The year 1979 signaled the start of a strong commercial construction boom, unusually strong even for the real estate industry. Construction more than doubled from 1979 to 1985, significantly increasing as a share of gross domestic product (see Garner (2015)). The inevitable bust potentially signaled an end to "business as usual." When analyzing economic data, it is important not only to examine how investment behavior affects the market, but also how the market affects investor behavior. How exactly do market drivers affect investment behavior and, furthermore, how is investor behavior altered after significant market events such as a recession? Sivitanidou and Sivitandes (2000) aim to expand on modern irreversible investment theories and to create an empirical model to help explain the effect of demand volatility on office-commercial construction, as well as to provide further empirical analysis for other determinants. They also shed light on the pre- and postrecessionary differences in investor response to demand volatility.

The authors utilize survey-based data compiled by CB Richard Ellis/ Torto Wheaton Research which took detailed inventory surveys of all buildings located within the chosen metropolitan boundaries that are 20,000 square feet or larger in size.

The theory of irreversible investments states that the significant irretrievable cost associated with undertaking an irreversible investment de-incentivizes investors from doing so. A project cannot be discontinued without cost to the investor. Of course if an investor had knowledge about their returns, the fact that the investment is irreversible wouldn't make a difference in their decisions or the project's value. The higher the irretrievable cost, the higher the potential threshold value investors require before they enter the market. The authors postulate that increased demand uncertainty further de-incentivizes investors from entering.

The authors' results were consistent with the theory that an increase in uncertainty de-incentivized office-commercial construction and increased the threshold return required to make an investment. Demand volatility was found to have a beta of –0.02. This means if demand uncertainty doubles (i.e., increases by 100 percent), then office commercial construction will fall by approximately 2 percent, which is a fairly weak effect. Although this was a significant effect, it paled in comparison to the beta of other determinants included in the analysis. More significant determinants of construction include rental income flows, the discount rate, office employment growth rate, land cost, and climate.

Although demand volatility showed weak influence over office-commercial construction rates in the prerecessionary period, its effects on investor behavior appeared to increase in the early 1990s postrecessionary period. Investors were then pricing in the possibility of a market collapse, which increased the threshold required for them to make an irreversible investment. Investors showed a weaker response to changes in the other determinants mentioned in the paper, namely the rental income flow and expected cash-flow growth. This again supports the notion of more cautionary investment behavior. The lag time between project initiation and completion decreased significantly from approximately 3 years to an average of 2.1. This suggests that developers were undertaking more favorable projects with shorter completion times as projects with longer completion times posed a higher risk, and that they may have been hesitant about the future state of the economy.

The importance of demand volatility on office-commercial construction appears to vary depending on the state of the economy and the current proximity to past recessions. In times of high market confidence, it appears to exert weak effects. In postrecessionary environments, its effect is amplified as investors exhibit more cautionary behavior and react less to other positive investment determinants.

Sivitanidou and Sivitandes' (2000) insights into irreversible investment theory may be particularly relevant for evaluating investment behavior as it relates to the post-2008 recession era. In their book *House of Debt*, Mian and Sufi explore the causes of The Great Recession and offer some data-supported theories as to why more and more low-credit low-income consumers were incentivized to invest in housing rather than rent. They suggest that an expansion in available credit and expectations about rising house prices may have played a part in fueling the housing bubble. Perhaps, consistent with Sivitanidou and Sivitandes (2000) findings on investments, potential homeowners are exhibiting more cautionary behavior and have experienced an increase in threshold value required for them to invest in homes. This could signal the end to "business as usual" when it comes to home ownership, consistent with the rising popularity of renting and increasing average age of first-time home buyers.

A potential weakness of Sivitanidou and Sivitandes (2000) is that once the authors acknowledge that the effect of irreversibility in investments is overshadowed by other factors, they continue treating it like it is the main factor, contrary to their previous claim. While it is understandable, one could argue that the subsequent expansion on the topic is unnecessary given the lower significance that investment irreversibility was found to have in comparison to other factors.

One could also question the effectiveness of Beta coefficients. Volatility obtained from betas are dependent on the past and are not necessarily accurate at predicting volatility of the future. Given the many noncyclical factors and triggers of the office-commercial office space market, it could be argued that Betas rely too heavily on historical data and previous structure of the economy to effectively be used for the present. So while the results may have presented a certain picture for the 1980s and 1990s, they might not be as applicable for other periods of extreme change in the office-commercial market. This would make an interesting further study. Following the 2008 recession, when investors were once again hesitant to invest, did investment irreversibility play a large role in their decisions?

Another factor that could be explored is investor responsiveness to government interventionist policies that aim to incentivize them to invest (policies such as expansionary monetary policy which made it cheaper for investors to take out loans for their projects). While the market was certainly shaken by the events of 2008, the subsequent dramatic drop in price of loans (interest rate) could have had a significant effect on the willingness of investors to invest in office-commercial space despite the potential risk. A potential further research point is whether the very low interest rate provided enough incentive for investors to invest, despite the uncertainty in the post-2008 recession economy.

Multiple Choice Questions

1. According to Sivitanidou's and Sivitandes (2000), which of the following is correct?
   a. **Modern investment theory proposes that in addition to those factors advocated by the deterministic q-theory, economic volatility influences the opportunity cost of irreversible investments, and as such, must also play a role in influencing investment decisions**
   b. Modern investment theory proposed that the only main factor that significantly influences investment decisions is the q-theory, which is a ratio comparing market value of firm capital to the replacement costs of firm physical assets
   c. Neither the modern investment theory nor the traditional investment theory take Tobin's q-theory into account in the context of real estate
   d. The only context in which one should take Tobin's q-theory into account is when determining whether or not to rebuild/repair lost or damaged assets

Explanation: Tobin's q-theory aims to determine whether or not it is in the best interest of a firm to invest in capital or sell it. It is a ratio of a firm's market value to the replacement cost of their physical assets. The traditional investment theory features this as the only main factor in determining if investment makes sense given certain circumstances. Modern investment theory (the main focus of this paper) introduces another factor into the mix: economic volatility. This is significant as in the context of office-space construction, investments are largely nonreversible, while the economy is growing more volatile.

2. Which of the following most accurately represents the conclusion drawn in Sivitanidou's and Sivitandes (2000), concerning demand volatility?

    a. Demand volatility is determined to be the single most significant factor of office-commercial construction

    b. **Demand volatility is determined to have a statistical significant effect on office-commercial construction. However, other factors are found to carry a more significant weight**

    c. Demand volatility is determined to have a statistically insignificant effect on office-commercial construction

    d. Demand volatility was not studied in this paper

Explanation: In their conclusion, Sivitanidou and Sivitanides comment on their empirical findings, stating demand volatility has an effect on office-commercial construction. This is consistent with the initial hypothesis of the paper. However, it is found that other factors have a larger effect on office-commercial construction, which was not initially accounted for.

3. According to Sivitanidou and Sivitandes (2000), when comparing the 1980s and 1990s, one can say that:

    a. **The office-market environment was significantly different in the 1990s from the 1980s. This caused uncertainty and hesitancy among investors, causing them to react less responsively to market conditions**

    b. The office-market environment thrived throughout the 1980s and 1990s, and thus investor responsiveness went up as time went on

    c. Only the 1980s were studied in this paper

    d. Hesitancy and responsiveness were determined not to be factors of/effects on the office-market environment throughout the 1980s and 1990s

Explanation: Following the crash, investors were unsure about the future of the housing market and the potential profitability of their irreversible investments, and they explored opportunity costs (the next best option that is forgone in favor of another economic decision) that could come with them. This lack of confidence led to a cautious mindset forming among investors, causing them to be less responsive to market changes, even when they were in their favor, because of the risk factor.

References

Garner, A. C. (2015), "Is Commercial Real Estate Reliving the 1980's and Early 1990's?" Federal Reserve Bank of Kansas City, Working Paper.

Mian, A. and A. Sufi (2014), "House of Debt," University of Chicago Press: Chicago, USA.

Sivitanidou, R. and P. Sivitanides (2000), "Does the Theory of Irreversible Investments Help Explain Movements in Office–Commercial Construction?" Real Estate Economics 28, 623–661.

PART VI

Selected Topics

CHAPTER 16

Contamination Risk

In collaboration with Grant Fitzgerald and Ross Williams

Over the past few years, there has been discussion whether the role of contamination risk and redevelopment are correlated. Contamination risk is defined as the risk being absorbed by a developer that is stemming from the environmental conditions of the property. Finding an answer to this question helps us understand the importance of quality environmental conditions on the behavior of urban development

Generally, there has been a large negative perception about contaminated property due to the large legal and financial barriers that they pose. This has a negative effect on the surrounding communities and creates a stagnant economic environment. This problem has led economists and real estate developers to suggest that municipalities take on some financial responsibility to encourage redevelopment of these contaminated parcels. Some suggest that this would make the cities more attractive for industrial users. McGrath (1996) seeks to discover whether the contamination risk of a property has an accurate impact on land value, and probability of redevelopment.

McGrath (1996) analyzes property data of the central business district of Chicago and its surrounding areas. The goals of the paper are to determine how potential property contamination in the form of land or structural contamination affects both the probability of commercial re-development and the price at which the land is valued. After establishing that the contamination probability was statistically significant, McGrath aims to find a solution to the larger problem of what alternatives could be taken to benefit both the developers and the local economy. McGrath focuses in on whether or not the data supports the local municipalities mitigating the risks of contamination of these properties in order to spur economic growth in their communities.

The primary data set used in this paper is a group of 195 redeveloped and current-use property sales from the City of Chicago from August 1983 through November 1993. This data was obtained from the City of Chicago's Harris-REDI database. The redeveloped property data subset is composed of 95 redeveloped industrial properties. These properties were determined as redeveloped if the parcel was purchased with an industrial demolition permit and/or had an industrial building permit within 24 months of the sale. The current-use subset is composed of 100 properties chosen randomly through the industrial sale record. These properties are zoned for manufacturing and have no permits for demolition or building. Together, both redevelopment and current-use types total 195 properties. All properties were assigned a historical land use that was determined by researching the 1949 and 1975 versions of the Sanborn Fire Insurance Maps. With these historical records, each land-use category could be assigned a probability of contamination.

The primary economic model used for this study was the "optimal redevelopment rule." Brueckner (1980) and Wheaton (1982) state, "the present value of revenue obtainable from a parcel converted to new use, net of capital development costs, must equal or exceed the present value of the gross revenue from the existing capital stock on the parcel." In other words a particular parcel should be redeveloped if the present value of the parcel in its new use is greater than the value of parcel in its current use. This rule is reinforced by Rosenthal and Helsey (1994) with the assumptions that landowners are myopic capital costs are constant, there is no structural depreciation, and that demolition costs are zero. Munneke (1996) decided to change the assumption of no demolition costs because if they were large enough the rule would not provide accurate information. Therefore, the rule, in this study, includes two demolition costs. The first is related to the existing structure and the second is related to the land and soil of the parcel.

The value differential for the properties is estimated through regression analysis with the data set. This regression analysis provides vectors of characteristics relating to redevelopment value and current-use value. This unbiased analysis provides an accurate value differential for each property in the data set.

McGrath (1996) found that investors would bid on properties that had contamination risks. Properties would still be redeveloped, but depending on their risk the values these properties would receive were significantly lower than a comparable property with a lower contamination risk. When bidding on these properties, investors would account for the risk of contamination and the costs associated with potential contamination by offering a lower bid. The discounts had a wide range of values, but the interesting result was that these values were often much larger than the actual cost of cleaning up the property. After analyzing the data, the observed discount per parcel varied between $400,000 and $800,000 most often. On average, Noonan and Vidich (1992) found that the actual cost to cleanup a property was only $290,000. These values leave money on the table that could be getting taxed to benefit the local economy, but instead are never spent because of the negative impact that site contamination poses.

The economic model also found that the probability of redevelopment was greatly dependent on the value differential associated with redevelopment. Contamination risk impacted this value differential because it caused the investor to have to invest more capital upfront leading to a lower return. It was found that the investor could recoup all of the costs associated with the contamination cleanup because the resulting increase in land value would compensate them for these expenditures.

A publicly funded cleanup could be justified especially for the marginal parcel. Looking at the characteristics of a property and its surrounding properties can identify a marginal parcel. If the property would normally be redeveloped barring the current contamination risk, then the city would benefit from using public money to clean up the site. By remediating the contamination risk of the average parcel, which previously had a 67 percent chance of contamination, the resulting increase in probability of redevelopment was 35 percent. By eliminating the contamination risk, the probability of redevelopment rose from a starting point of 57 percent all the way up to 92 percent. These average parcels only began with a value differential of $192,000.

When taking into account which properties to publicly fund a cleanup for, the municipalities should focus on the marginal parcel. It has been shown that many properties will still be redeveloped even with the risk of contamination, but properties in desirable locations that are not being developed because of their underlying contamination risk are the ones that hold the greatest potential benefit from the city eliminating the contamination risk. Given that the economy would benefit from the financial effects of redevelopment occurring as well as the positive health benefits for the community from eliminating contamination issues, the paper supports the idea that there is an opportunity for a publicly funded cleanup to make a substantial positive impact on the local community.

McGrath (1996) uses multiple regression analysis to provide evidence that a publicly funded cleanup may be justified. McGrath focuses on the statistically relevant factors such as proximity to the central business district, population density, and the past uses of the parcel to determine an expected parcel value with and without the liability of contamination. The benefits associated with this cleanup are briefly touched upon, but there is not enough detail given to show the magnitude of the impact that would result from a publicly funded cleanup. Further research and continued expansion on the new value being created would help to clarify just how important the remediation of Chicago's marginal parcels could be.

Improving the marginal property, so that it would be redeveloped, would bring in more jobs and additional tax dollars, but other analyses are needed to determine the entirety of the effect that this would bring to the local economies. The paper does a good job of establishing that the data supports an opportunity for the local economies to benefit from a publicly funded cleanup, but a local economy would want to see a more in-depth analyses before proceeding to remedy the contamination issues.

Multiple Choice Questions

1. According to McGrath (1996), if a property was bid at a higher discount than the actual cost of cleanup:
   a. The property is assessed at a higher value
   b. **The property brings in less taxes for the municipality**
   b. The property brings in more taxes for the municipality
   c. (a) and (c) are both correct

Explanation: The correct answer is (b). The bids for the property determine what the market value of the property is. A higher discount means the bid for the property is too low in comparison to the cleanup costs. A smaller discount means the bid for the property was too high in comparison to the cleanup costs. If a property was bid at a higher discount than the cost of cleanup, real estate appraisers are valuing the property too low. Therefore, the property will bring in less taxes for the municipality than if it were to be bid at the proper discount (one equal to the cost of cleanup).

2. According to McGrath, the marginal parcel is defined as follows:
   a. A parcel of land that would not receive a loan without the expansion of credit
   b. A parcel of land that would not be redeveloped without a publicly funded cleanup
   c. A parcel of land that has contamination risk, but is located in a desirable spot for redevelopment
   d. **(b) and (c) are both correct**

Explanation: The correct answer is (d). Both answers (b) and (c) are correct. A marginal parcel is defined as a piece of land that is not currently being redeveloped because of the underlying contamination risk. Once that risk is eliminated through a publicly funded clean up, the parcel is then redeveloped because not only is the parcel in a desirable location, but it also no longer holds contamination risk. Choice (a) is incorrect because that is referring to a marginal borrower and in this case we are looking for the definition of a marginal parcel.

3. According to McGrath (1996), if municipalities were to subsidize contamination cost of cleanup for industrial properties:
   a. More jobs would be created due to increased redevelopment
   b. Tax revenue would increase due to higher appraisal values
   c. Tax revenue would decrease due to lower appraisal values
   d. **Both (a) and (b) are correct**

Explanation: The correct answer is (d). This study concludes that the market was overestimating the contamination costs for the industrial parcels. Therefore the local appraisers undervalued the land. If the local government paid for the contamination costs, the costs of cleanup would be public information and known to be relatively lower than expected cost. This would lead to a higher appraisal values and higher tax revenue for the city. In addition, if the city was to subsidize the contamination costs, the probability of redevelopment is higher and would lead to more jobs.

References

Noonan, F. and C. A. Vidich (1992), "Decision analysis for utilizing hazardous waste site assessments in real estate acquisition," Risk Analysis 12, 245–251.

Rosenthal, S. S. and R. W. Helsley (1994), "Redevelopment and the urban land price gradient," Journal of Urban Economics 35, 182–200.

Mian, A. and A. Sufi (2014), "House of Debt," University of Chicago Press: Chicago, USA.

McGrath, D (1996), "Urban Industrial Land Redevelopment and Contamination Risk," Journal of Urban Land Economics 47, 414–442.

Wheaton, W. C. (1982), "Urban Spatial Development with Durable but Replaceable Capital," Journal of Urban Economics 12, 53–67.

Brueckner, J. K. (1980), "A vintage model of urban growth," Journal of Urban Economics 8, 389–402.

Munneke, H. J. (1996), "Redevelopment Decisions for Commercial and Industrial Properties," Journal of Urban Economics 39, 229–253.

CHAPTER 17

Land Prices and Uncertainty

In collaboration with Shreya Mittal and Jonathan Laws

How have house prices fluctuated in the different regions in the United States over the last 30 years? Which factor has had the biggest effect on house price fluctuations and with these findings? What is the future outlook for this factor's impact on house prices? The goal of Davis and Palumbo (2008) is to answer these questions by analyzing and comparing how house prices in large metropolitan areas of the United States have fluctuated between 1984 and 2004, and finding reasons for the results. In addition, the paper uses their findings to predict the future path of house prices in these cities.

In the year 1998, the United States experienced some of the best economic conditions in history, which included a large growth in real GDP and a significant rise in real wages. Also during this time, the majority of metropolitan cities in the United States experienced a rapid increase in value of land, which increased the land's share of home value significantly. However, the rise in value varied greatly from region to region, as land represented about 81 percent of average single-family home value in San Francisco, whereas land represented only 33 percent of home value in Milwaukee. In fact, since 1998, the large cities in the Midwest, Southeast, and Southwest have seen steady increases in real average home values of 25 percent, when in comparison, cities along the East and West coast, such as San Francisco, have seen an astronomical increase in real land value of 80 percent. Davis and Palumbo (2008) discuss this difference in the price and value of residential land for 46 large metropolitan U.S. cities from 1984 to 2004 and try to find some explanations for their results.

The authors use data from various sources, including databases used by Davis and Heathcote (2007) and Fraumeni (1997) to achieve their goals for this research. Other data, such as changes in components of home value by geographic region (from 1984 to 1998), changes in components of home value by geographic region (from 1999 to 2004), and effect of higher land share on prospective home-price appreciation, are all derived from the American Housing Survey (AHS). An explicit equation is also used to express growth in land prices as a weighted average of growth in construction costs and growth in home prices. Deriving data for the changes in home prices from "Freddie Mac's Conventional Home Price Index" (CMPHI) and changes and levels of construction costs from "R.S Means company," Davis and Palumbo then estimate the land prices by putting these values into the original equation. While doing so, they also discover that land's share of new homes is less than land's share of the average existing home. These calculations and conclusions are drawn with the assumption that land doesn't depreciate and the depreciation rate of the structures is taken as a constant of 1.5 percent. Another outcome of these calculations is seen as it was noted that land's share of home value increased from 34 percent to 46 percent in Minneapolis–St. Paul, whereas in San Francisco the share increased sharply from 13 percent to 88 percent. Scrutinizing this data, Davis and Palumbo suggest that one would expect land prices to move closely with construction costs where land is inexpensive and prices are stable (e.g., Minneapolis–St. Paul), whereas one can expect the price of land to appreciate rapidly if home prices outpace construction costs (e.g., San Francisco).

Davis and Palumbo use all the data and algorithms that they have found regarding the components of home value and the changes in home value primarily from 1984 to 2004 to derive conclusions. The results are deduced for the 46 large cities in the United States by grouping them into five broad geographical regions. It is seen that the difference in the value of residential land across regions was the fundamental reason for the different home prices in different regions. This holds true despite the difference in the average replacement cost of structures. The data validates this conclusion as, at the end of 1984, residential land alone accounted for 11 percent of home value in Midwest cities and 55 percent along the West coast. This rise in the value of home prices continued throughout 2004, when land's share of home value rose to 74 percent along the west coast compared to 55 percent in 1984, and 36 percent in Midwest cities compared to 11 percent in 2004. Although the average land's share of home value rose to 51 percent by the end of 2004, it is clear that land in east and west coasts was much more expensive as compared to other regions such as the Midwest, Southwest, and Southeast.

As a result of an appreciation in residential land, homes became more valuable in all four regions except the Southwest. The rising land values allowed for an increase in the real terms of the residential land by 50 percent from 1984 to 1998, increasing the land's share of home value to 40 percent. From 1999 to 2004, changes in the real values of home were on a rapid pace. The authors estimate that the surge in residential land was about 50 percent in the Southeast and Southwest, 75 percent in the Midwest and roughly 125 percent in the East and West coast, after adjusting for inflation.

Davis and Palumbo extend their results and show how major cities in all five regions have also experienced a lengthened and prominent decline in real land values in the late 1980s and 1990s, which was shortly before there were rapid increases in real house prices. The paper gives the example of Houston, where real prices fell cumulatively by 50 percent for 5 years until 1989 and, although prices began to rise, it took Houston 15 years to return to the price level it was in 1985. Davis and Palumbo also show how 30 other cities (excluding the Southwest region) reached a local peak sometime after 1986, out of which 15 cities have experienced a 3-year decline of net 16 percent or more in real land prices. Some cities out of the 30 failed to reach their 1990 peak until the housing boom in the 2000s. Davis and Palumbo also point out that the decline in real land prices caused a stagnation of land prices in nominal terms, which contrasted with a rise in consumer prices, causing a large increase in the consumer price index over time.

After analyzing all the results and data points, it is evident that most U.S. large metropolitan cities have experienced a price cycling since 1980s, in which the real residential land prices reached a peak and were then succeeded by a long period of recovery. As the paper formulates price index for residential land, it concludes further that, for the most part, the majority of large cities in the United States have seen a significant rise in average price and value of land, both on real and nominal basis. Another conclusion that can be drawn from looking at the data is that the East and West coast experienced a greater overall increase in real and nominal residential land values as compared to other regions such as the Southwest, Southeast, and Midwest. Also that the main driver of these increases in residential land values is the value of the actual land and not the physical structures that exist on the property. This, they conclude, is due to demand-based increases, such as increased demand for property in the catchment area of good public schools and public parks, and so on.

Davis and Palumbo also accentuate and touch upon the concept of how elasticity of supply of housing affects the land's share of home value. Davis and Palumbo use a stylized housing supply curve, which represents two regions; region 1 and region 2. The graph shown levels out in region 1, but then it begins to steep upwards in region 2. David and Palumbo explain this pattern of the graph by categorizing region 1 as elastic housing supply, with abundant, inexpensive land with replacement cost of houses accounting for the major part of home values. Although they categorize region 2 as inelastic housing supply where land is more scarce, making it relatively more expensive and increasing the land's share of housing, and decreasing the elasticity of the supply of housing. Davis and Palumbo then go on to strengthen this point with data showing that market value of residential land was 50 percent in the Southeast and Southwest (region 1, where land is abundant hence inexpensive) and around 125 percent in the East and West coasts (region 2, where land is scarce and more expensive). This result connects well with Mian and Sufi (2014) where they argue that cities with unlimited flat terrain have elastic housing supply as new houses can be quickly built when demand increases and house prices rise. In this case, cities in the Southeast, Midwest, and Southwest, where prices didn't rise as much, can be classified as having an elastic housing supply. However, according to Mian and Sufi, cities which are restricted by water bodies or hills have inelastic housing supply, as the supply cannot respond quickly enough to prices surges. In the case of the United States, the East and West coast cities have inelastic housing supply due to geographical restrictions. Connecting Mian and Sufi's research and their findings with Davis and Palumbo (2008) validates the data even further as to why the East and West coast saw the greatest upsurge.

Davis and Palumbo define a home's value as a sum of the replacement cost of its structure and the market value of the land and location. They use a constant depreciation rate of 1.5 percent per year in accordance with data from the Bureau of Economic Analysis (BEA) to all Metropolitan Statistical Areas (MSAs). This can be seen as a weakness of the paper as depreciation rates may vary according to the vintage structures, different periods of time and are also dependent on the age of structure (i.e., a house). If this 1.5 percent depreciation rate is used to calculate all the land prices and land's share of home values throughout 1984 to 2004, then the data could be off the mark. That is, if depreciation rate was raised to 3 percent, land's share of home value would increase and the growth rate of land prices would decrease. Further research on this would be needed. Davis and Palumbo also suggest a correlation between the rise in land prices from 1998 and the rise of land prices in the future. They extend the idea, proposing that land's greater share in home value could mean more rapid price appreciation of land and larger swings in home prices, particularly when housing is becoming relatively inelastic in most regions. Davis and Palumbo also suggest that even if land prices were to rise on an average pace as before the housing boom, one could still expect a large increase in the home prices much more quickly. Further research on this topic can help offer a greater insight as to how much change in house prices can be expected due to the rise in land price at the present time.

Multiple Choice Questions

1. According to Davis and Palumbo (2008), which component in the housing bundle accounts the most for the increases in value of property in large metropolitan areas?
   a. The physical structure (the building)
   b. **The land**
   c. Replacement cost of buildings
   d. Changes in zoning regulations

Explanation: The correct answer is (c). Between 1984 and 2004, Davis and Palumbo come to the conclusion that house prices have increased drastically due to the housing becoming much more land intensive. This means that demand factors are the cause for the price increases, and are likely to be the reason for land price increases in the future. Although the physical structure built on the land has an effect on house prices, it does not account to a large extent for the price increases that have been experienced in these large metropolitan areas. The reason for the price increase through demand factors is because people are increasingly valuing the location of the land, due to factors such as: catchment area for good schools, upper end shops, reputation of the neighborhood, and not what the land actually is. The extent of the land's impact on the price is greater in regions that are inelastic, such as the West coast, because there is less room to build other houses due to geographical limitations, while elastic regions, such as the Midwest, have plenty of room for housing supply expansion.

2. According to Davis and Palumbo (2008), which region out of the five showed the greatest increase in real average home values since 1998?

   a. Midwest

   b. Southeast

   c. Southwest

   d. **East and West coast**

Explanation: The correct answer is (d). Although all regions in the United States have seen a substantial real increase in the average home values, the East and West coasts have experienced an astronomical rise of 80 percent (cumulatively). This is seen as the construction costs have surpassed consumer price inflation, causing the real value of residential land to rise from 10 to 18 percent since 1998. As the value of residential land increases in real terms, the land's share of home value increases along with it (about 13 to 18 percentage points in the East and West coasts). In addition, the rapid appreciation in real land prices causes the average home value to increase both in nominal and real terms. This is caused, once again, by demand factors, as the East and West Coast have an inelastic housing supply, which makes creation of new housing a difficult task.

3. According to Davis and Palumbo (2008), what is a consequence if residential land accounts for a greater share of home value?

   a. **Increases land price volatility**

   b. Causes a decrease in the home value

   c. Stagnates the price of houses

   d. Increases the "accounting effect"

Explanation: The correct answer choice is (a). According to the calculations done by Davis and Palumbo the more expensive land values currently in place can cause real home prices to accelerate by more than 1 percentage point per year in cities along the coasts. They also note that even if land prices were to rise by an average rate, home prices are expected to rise more rapidly as compared to before. This quick and rapid rise in house prices allows for a greater swing in land prices and hence increases the land price volatility in large metropolitan cities (especially along the East and West coast cities) where land is already inelastically supplied and is much more expensive than other regions.

References

Davis, M. A. and M. G. Palumbo (2008), "The Price of Residential Land in Large US Cities," Journal of Urban Economics 63, 352–384.

Davis, M. and J. Heathcote (2007), "The Price and Quantity of Residential Land Prices in the United States," Journal of Monetary Economics 54, 2595–2620.

Fraumeni B. (1997), "The Measurement of Depreciation in the US National Income and Product Accounts," Survey of Current Business 2, 7–23.

Mian, A. and A. Sufi (2014), "House of Debt," The University of Chicago Press: Chicago, USA.

CHAPTER 18

Housing Affordability

In collaboration with Yi Li and Brian Zage

Affordable housing is a topic that is debated constantly among American policy makers. The implications of affordable housing and providing for the homeless cannot be understated, as millions of people require these services in order to survive. While great strides have been made in terms of offering help to those who need it, our country still faces this very serious and very real problem.

Homelessness has always been an issue in the United States, and has become a problem that government entities have tried to remedy. Policy makers have been tasked with the job of finding a way to successfully approach the problem while finding effective ways to eliminate or reduce the amount of homeless people that exist. Considering each individual in this world is born into a different situation, how do we determine who needs the most help and which people to target for affordable housing?

The U.S. Department of Housing and Urban Development as well as other agencies and organizations have all studied these variables to attempt to reduce the amount of people in our country who are homeless. While some have been successful in doing this, there are still a large amount of people who are not being provided with the support and aid that they need and warrant. In his study, Early (2004) attempts to further understand the causes of homelessness by finding the largest determinants and measuring how well current housing assistance programs are at addressing these issues.

When choosing who is eligible for different types of programs that are offered to the homeless and the poor, many variables are taken into account such as gender, family size, income level, and age. Policy has been created to target those in need, but the question of how well these policies are doing remains. Therefore, the goal of this study is to address how successful these policies are by figuring out if those who need assistance the most are actually getting it. Early (2004) was able to do this by studying poor households and the probability of homelessness among them. Combining this with information on those poor families who are in subsidized housing, we can then see how many families would become homeless without the assistance of their subsidy.

The study combines data from previous studies and other separate surveys to generate samples of homelessness and low-income households under unsubsidized renting housing. A logit regression is used to determine the probability of being homeless as a function of characteristics of households and the areas the households are located. Then the author simulates the results of the regression to a sample of households who are currently under subsidized programs to estimate the fraction of households who would be homeless under the absence of the subsidy. Observations of homelessness and poor households under unsubsidized housing are from the 1996 National Survey of Homelessness Assistance Providers and Clients (NSHAPC), and data was collected through 22 largest metropolitan areas. Finally, Early (2004) incorporates 1418 observations on homeless and 2069 observations on poor households in unsubsidized rental housing. In order to test the effectiveness of the current subsidy program, 540 observations of households under subsidized housing are drawn from SIPP and NSHAPC data sets. Early (2004) furthers the study by taking endogeneity of income into consideration. He applies a two-stage estimation model in control of how endogeneity of income would affect the result.

The three variables of household markets included in the regression model are price of substandard rental housing, the lowest rate needed to occupy a rental unit, and the vacancy rate of low cost housing. As there are no sources of these variables existing, the author uses a hedonic model as a function of structural characteristics of house unit, measure of unit quality, and neighborhood to estimate these variables.

Other area-specific variables included are measures of average level of aid directed toward low-income households, max AFDC benefit, amount spent per personal served by community health care clinics, and shortage of mental health care. The author believes all these factors are necessary to consider in the regression model. Further, Early (2004) put household-specific variables into consideration. These variables are income, household size, gender, race and ethnicity, age and head of the household. While inclusion of the above factors is obvious, Early (2004) has special interest in whether Vietnam veteran status is a factor. He believes Vietnam veterans are underrepresented in homelessness studies.

Due to the potential endogeneity of income, there are three specifications of the model that are presented. Model 1 assumes income is exogenous, Model 2 treats income as endogenous and employs a two-stage process to estimate the model, and Model 3 is a reduced form regression. Early (2004) substituted the equation explaining income for the equation explaining homelessness to remove income from the regression and add the explanatory variables used in the income equation. Therefore, when running the logit regressions, we are able to see the variables being studied and their levels of significance among all three models.

The findings were consistent among the three different modifications. Households headed by women and headed by persons more than 50 years of age were less likely to be homeless. Also, it was found that African-Americans are more likely to be homeless, when everything else was held constant. States with higher per capita spending on community health care resulted in less households likely to be homeless. Average minimum temperature was inversely related to the probability of being homeless, which surprised the researchers. While one would think the housing market in a given location would play a large role in homelessness, only vacancy rates for low rent units in the reduced form regression was a statistically significant factor. All of the other variables used to describe conditions of the housing market were not significant in the study.

After this initial analysis, Early (2004) moves the research to the next level, providing the predicted probability of being homeless of a hypothetical low-income household. As certain variables such as monthly income, age, married, and Vietnam veteran are changed, the numbers adjust and the percent change in the probability of being homeless fluctuates. The research shows that with other variables being held constant, changes in demographic characteristics largely influence the predicted probability of the household being homeless. Marital status, income, gender, and race were the variables with a strong pull, while variables such as increasing the price of substandard housing and rental vacancy rates for low-cost housing did not have much pull.

In conclusion, the study shows that female-headed households, households with older heads, and nonminority households are less likely to be homeless. This result mirrors the study done in mid-1980s. The simulation of results of the regression model compared to the current households under subsidized programs indicates that housing authorities do not target those who are at the most risk of being homeless. Early (2004) states that while men make up a large fraction of homeless population, housing subsidy programs tend to support households with children. Moreover, those who are at most risk to be homeless tend to have alcohol and drug addiction problems. This would limit chances of being subsidized. The author asserts that housing authorities should do more to target those who are at most risk of being homeless without relaxing the support on families with children. Early (2004) argues that the current income eligibility for being subsidized is too strict and that it does not effectively target those who are at the most risk of being homeless. According to Early (2004), based on setting preferences used for housing authorities to select who should receive assistance, nothing should prevent them from targeting those who are most likely to be homeless in the absence of subsidy. However, the fact is that 27 percent of housing staff authorities tend to assist people who are in school, working, and under job training programs, and less than 12 percent of them follow the hardship measurements of the selecting process. Early (2004) finally assists that the federal guidelines should require housing authorities to target the poorest of the poor households, and that income eligibility requirements should be lowered.

In their book, *House of Debt*, Mian and Sufi (2014) investigate reasons causing the great recession. They insisted that the subprime mortgage market crash in 2007 caused deep reduction in household spending, which induced the great recession. They also demonstrate the concentration losses on debtors and the amplification effect due to foreclosure. A lot of people became unemployed and had become homeless without housing subsidies during the great recession. Before the Great Recession,

Early (2004) argued that the targeting of housing assistance is not sufficient because the minimum income requirement is too strict. Therefore, after the Great Recession, this only becomes more true as millions of jobs were lost, and the average median income level among the lower class was only further reduced.

Early (2004) mentions several data limitations which would bias or underestimate the results. According to Early (2004), the NSHAPC gathered data on homelessness at one point of time instead of a period of time. This fails to indicate households who would remain homeless in the near future. Also, the one-point prevalence of homelessness would underestimate the effectiveness of the subsidy program. Furthermore, studies tend to sample those who spend a long time being homeless, and these households are inclined to associate with certain factors (severe chemical addiction and problem with mental illness). This disproportion of data would be biased to show a strong relationship between homelessness and these certain factors. Furthermore, the one-point prevalence targeting of homelessness would underestimate the effectiveness of current subsidized programs. Moreover, the author suggests that the length of duration households have received housing subsidy may alter characteristics of households. Since no such measure is included in this study, further possibilities could not be explored.

Research should be conducted to show the timetables of the families in question, and how often they slip in and out of homelessness. The data that Early (2004) analyzed does not take into account how volatile the life of a homeless family can be. More studies can be done to measure how successful affordable housing programs and subsidized housing are at keeping families off the streets in the long term. Appropriately so, many housing programs are targeted at supporting families who have dependent children. Unfortunately, this prevents many young-adult men from getting the assistance they need. Often removed from their homes for a variety of reasons, young men have the tendency of getting lost in the process. Therefore, future research should also take into consideration these nonelderly men who are forced to provide for themselves, and can determine a way to create better programs for them with the hopes of possibly saving their lives.

Multiple Choice Questions

1. Through the study, Early (2004), which households were found to be less likely of being homeless?
   a. Households headed by women
   b. Households headed by persons over the age of 50
   c. Households headed by young men
   d. **Both (a) and (c) are correct**
   d. All of the above

Explanation: The correct answer to this question is (d). Through the regression, the study found that households who were headed by women and headed by persons over the age of 50 were less likely to be homeless. Surveys have found that the most dependable households are those who are headed by older adults, while women have also been found to be more dependent than men. Many housing programs are targeted at providing households of families with children with assistance and aid, which has made them less likely of being homeless than those households made up of single young men.

2. According to Early (2004), which of the following explains why housing authorities fail to target those who are at the most risk of being homeless in the absence of subsidized housing?
   a. The income eligibility requirements set by housing subsidy programs is higher than median annual income of homeless families
   b. They tend to target those with severe alcohol and drug use
   c. They have preference to subsidy households who are working or are in school and under job training
   d. All of the above
   e. **Only (a) and (c) are correct**

Explanation: The right answer is (e). Only (a) and (c) are correct. The author mentions in the article that federal guideline for eligibility for public housing and Housing Choice Voucher Program is defined to be less than 80 percent of area median income. Recent legislation has taken consideration of extreme low-income households, and the requirement is set to be less than 30 percent of area median income. However, the median income of homeless is much lower than defined limit of even extremely low income in 22 metro areas, which makes harder for those who are at most risk to be homeless to receive assistance. (b) is not correct, because severe alcohol and drug use actually confound housing authorities in targeting these households who are most risk of being homeless. (c) is correct, as less than 13 percent of housing authorities follow hardship measurements of who should be assisted and who should be not. They tend to subsidy those who are in school or at work and under job training, believing they are worth subsidizing.

3. According to Early (2004), all of the following variables played a large role in determining homelessness EXCEPT:
   a. **Variables describing conditions of the housing market**
   b. States with high per capita spending on community health care
   c. Monthly household income
   d. Household size
   e. Both (a) and (d) are correct

Explanation: The answer is (a), variables describing conditions of the housing market. While we would think that the housing market plays a very large role in determining homelessness, this is not entirely the case. The problem does not simply lie with the amount of affordable housing that is offered, but is more related to whom the subsidized housing is offered to. The regression shows that (b), (c), and (d) are all variables that are statistically significant in determining homelessness, while variables associated with the housing market are not.

References

Mian, A. and A. Sufi (2014), "House of Debt," University of Chicago Press: Chicago, USA.

Early, D. (2004), "The Determinants of Homelessness and the Targeting of Housing Assistance," Journal of Urban Economics 55, 195–214.

CHAPTER 19

Public Infrastructures

In collaboration with Matt Cain and Sara Werbeckes

Air travel has far-reaching indirect and direct effects on regional economies. Approximately two million people take commercial flights every day, and a large fraction of consumer products are transported by airplanes. Cities with large populations create and use these products every day to function effectively. Understanding the role that air transport plays in economies can help us gain insight on how infrastructure affects economic growth.

Do some citizens in these large populations create environments for airports to develop, or does the development of airports lead to an increase in population? This classic chicken or the egg problem is what Richard K. Green tries to solve in his paper, Green (2007). In this paper, Green tries to distinguish whether the building of airports creates large population and economic growth in a city or whether large population and economic growth lead to the building of airports in cities. Separating these closely linked elements is not an easy task. However, by taking other related variables out of the equation, it is easier to see a relationship form. These variables include airport measures such as boardings and originations along with economic measures such as percent of workforce in FIRE industries (Financial, Insurance, and Real Estate) in the surrounding city.

Green used many different sets of data while taking control variables into account. The data set used by far the most throughout the paper was the 1990 census of population and housing. This data set was used when factoring in population of MSAs, property, corporate, and income tax rates, amount of population over 25 years of age with a high school diploma, with a college degree, the average commuting time, and if the state was a right-to-work state. Information from the Federal Aviation Administration was used to find the 100 largest airports in the United

States. No airport outside this list of 100 was used, as they were assumed too small to have an economic impact. These two data sets were combined (specifically the population portion of the 1990 census) to show boardings per capita for each of these airports. Climate factors for each MSA were taken into account by using average heating and cooling days as stated by the National Oceanic and Atmospheric Administration. County Business Patterns provided information on the percentages of employment in an MSA working in manufacturing and those in FIRE industries. They chose these specific industries because during the 1990s their shares grew unalike. The FIRE sector grew much more quickly during this time than the manufacturing sector.

Green's model uses a two-equation system to determine if there is any correlation between airport measures and economic measures. Green also adds other variables to the equations to see if there is a correlation between airport activity and the percent of the regional population over age 25 with a high school diploma, for example. The four main variables that Green tests are: boardings per capita, originations per capita, cargo per capita, and hub status. The model then tests these four variables against a multitude of variables ranging from distance from Kansas City to percent of workforce in manufacturing to per capita income. Where Green finds a high correlation between population growth or economic growth and one of the variables in the model, he determines that variable to be statistically significant. Those variables that are identified as statistically significant are then used to help describe population and economic growth. The economic intuition behind this method is that there must be a cause and effect relationship for population and economic growth and Green is trying to figure out if airport activity could be a cause in the cause and effect relationship for population and economic growth.

Green finds that boardings per capita and originations per capita are good predictors, in the country's largest metropolitan areas, of population and economic growth. Both boardings per capita and originations per capita have very large correlation coefficients. The magnitude of the coefficient on boardings per capita strongly implies that passenger boardings predictability on population growth and economic growth could be quite sizeable. Originations per capita also has a very large correlation coefficient which would indicate that originations per capita is also a solid predictor of population and economic growth. Green's model does an excellent job of finding out which variables might play a role in population and economic growth. In the end, Green finds that airport activity, particularly boarding per capita and originations per capita are good predictors of population and economic growth. Green's finding is not necessarily surprising because airports are essential in allowing people to move freely and easily between different metropolitan areas.

Green concludes that there is a relationship between boardings per capita and originations per capita, and population and economic growth, but does not suggest that every city work on building and airport to increase economic activity. The model Green uses works well for large metropolitan areas because the sheer number of people are that much larger than a small town, and the current amount of people and their use of the airport could be an underlying factor in population and economic growth. At the time of writing, Green's article was one of the first experiments of its kind done. This suggests that more work should be done to better foster the relationship between boardings and originations per capita and economic growth. Airports are controversial issues for communities, which Green addresses, and although Green's research shows a relationship between airport activity and economic growth, Green concludes that it might be difficult for larger metropolitan areas to increase their airport capacity to increase airport activity thus increasing economic growth. The difficulty arises in people of the community where the airport is located that would be against increased airport activity in their neighborhood. Green's work is significant because it sheds light on the role that airport activity plays in economic growth, and might help prove to some people that airports help drive more than just the tourism statistics in an area.

House of Debt by Atif Mian and Amir Sufi (2014) focuses on the collapse of the housing market during 2008, but also tries to explain patterns of behavior in society in the time before the 2008 crisis to find a valid reason for why it occurred and how we can prevent it from happening again in the future. In the 1990s, there was large economic growth in the United States due to the change in attitude toward debt. Credit was expanding and citizens were spending more on houses, goods, and more.[1] Green states in his paper that the reason they used FIRE sector jobs as a control variable was because this industry grew wildly fast in the 1990s

---

[1]Mian, A. and A. Sufi (2014), *House of Debt*, The University of Chicago Press.

(the main time frame of the paper) compared to other industries, such as manufacturing. An increase in the amount of people employed in these higher paying FIRE sector jobs and the expansion of credit led to an economic boom that seems sustainable in the long run. At least, that is what people wanted to believe.

Green's article is very strong, but there are a few weaknesses that could be addressed in future research. The idea of airport activity and growth leading to increased population and economic growth might just be a circle. Population growth and economic growth could be the leading indicators toward airport growth and thus activity. Green does not go into much depth about how or if population and economic in the 1980s was a driver for airport growth and activity. Metropolitan areas that experienced large population and economic growth could be the same areas that experienced high airport growth and activity in the early 1990s. If an area has experienced significant population and economic growth, it is foreseeable that airport activity and growth could increase as a result of the high population and economic growth. An analysis of population and economic growth figures from the 1980s in those metropolitan areas with the highest airport activity levels in the early 1990s would have helped strengthen Green's point. Green's article uses data from the early 1990s to form a connection between airport activity and levels of population and economic growth. The article lacks more current data that would help to show if the correlation between airport activity and population and economic growth is consistent for a period after the early 1990s. An analysis of more current data along with the data from the early 1990s would increase the reliability of the findings that in larger metropolitan areas high levels of airport activity have a strong correlation with population and economic growth. Green addresses that when the article was written there had not been a lot of research on this particular area of population and economic growth indicators. Although not his fault, having more previous research to work from would help increase the strength of Green's conclusions.

Green's paper was on the first of its kind which leaves wide open opportunities for more research in the field. Updated information is one way to see if trends are continuing into the 21st century. By having more information from the early 2000s we will have a wider, more accurate sample from which to pull information and find trends. Airport activity changed radically in 2001 after the attacks on the World Trade Center in New York City. Air traffic would never be the same again. Transportation Security Administration (TSA) regulations became harsher making it more of a hassle for regular travelers. The shock of the attacks also frightened those who do not normally fly making them not willing to risk taking a flight. Although the attacks were a major shock the airport industry might skew the numbers for the few years after the attacks, it would be interesting to run a similar regression again with data from the 2000s and 2010s.

Multiple Choice Questions

1. Which variables did Green (2007) find to be statistically significant in predicting population and economic growth?
   a. Presence of an NFL team.
   b. Number of hot and cold days
   c. **Originations per capita and boardings per capita**
   d. Distance from Kansas City

Explanation: The correct answer is (c): Green (2007) finds that originations per capita and boardings per capita are good predictors of population and economic growth. Originations per capita and boardings per capita have high test statistic values are highly correlated with population growth and economic growth. Green finds that the number of hot and cold days and the distance from Kansas City are not statistically significant variables in his regression model. The presence of an NFL team is never mentioned by Green in his article.

2. Does Green (2007) suggest that every city run out and build an airport to increase population and economic growth?
   a. Yes, of course they should!
   b. **No, Green does not suggest that every city run out and build an airport**
   c. Yes, but only if the airport cost is less than 50 million dollars
   d. No, because airports are eyesores

Explanation: The correct answer is (b): Green (2007) does not suggest that every city run out and build an airport because the data does not support airport activities correlation with population and economic growth in all types of metropolitan areas. Green never talks about the specific cost of airports only that they are very costly to build. Green does not specifically say anything about airports being eyesores, although he does comment on the fact that neighbors could be against increasing an airport's size because they can be a noise and traffic nuisance.

3. What source did Green (2007) use in his paper that provided the most information on the control variables?

   a. **The 1990 census of population and housing**

   b. The Federal Aviation Administration

   b. Because the work was one of the first of its kind, Green collected all of the information himself

   c. County Business Patterns

Explanation: The correct answer is (a): The source most used for information on the control variables was the 1990 census of population and housing. The Federal Aviation Administration only provided the list of largest MSAs. The County Business Patterns only provided the percentages of workers in the manufacturing industry and the percentage of workers in the FIRE industry. Although the work was one of the first of its kind, Green did not find all of the information by himself. It would have been incredibly difficult unreasonable to not use trusted outside sources for correct information.

References

Mian, A. and A. Sufi (2014), "House of Debt," University of Chicago Press: Chicago, USA.

Green, R. K. (2007), "Airports and Economic Development," Real Estate Economics 35, 91–112.

Bibliography

Baldi, F. (2013), "Valuing a Greenfield Real Estate Property Development Project: A Real Options Approach," Journal of European Real Estate Research 6, 186–217.

Belliot, J. and H. C. Smith (1981), "The Coastal Construction Control Line: A Cost-Benefit Analysis," AREUEA Journal.

Brueckner, J. K. (1980), "A Vintage Model of Urban Growth," Journal of Urban Economics 8, 389–402.

Bulan, L., C. Mayer and C. T. Somerville (2009), "Irreversible Investment, Real Options, and Competition: Evidence from Real Estate Development," Journal of Urban Economics 65, 247–251.

Burge, G. and K. Ihlanfeldt (2006), "Impact Fees and Single-Family Home Construction," Journal of Urban Economics 60, 284–306.

Burns, L. and L. Grebler (1982), "Construction Cycles in the United States Since World War II," Real Estate Economics 10, 123–151.

California Department of Conservation (1992), "Farmland Mapping and Monitoring Program. Sacramento County Important Farmland Map 1990," California Department of Conservation: Sacramento, California.

Cunningham, C. (2007), "Growth Controls, Real Options, and Land Development," Review of Economics and Statistics 89, 343–358.

Davis, M. A. and M. G. Palumbo (2008), "The Price of Residential Land in Large US cities," Journal of Urban Economics 63, 352–384.

Davis, M. and J. Heathcote (2007), "The Price and Quantity of Residential Land Prices in the United States," Journal of Monetary Economics 54, 2595–2620.

DiPasquale, D. and W. C. Wheaton (1994), "Housing Market Dynamics and the Future of Housing Prices," Journal of Urban Economics 35, 1–28.

Downs, A. (2004), "Growth Management and Affordable Housing: Do They Conflict?" Brookings Institution Press: Washington, D.C.

Early, D. (2004), "The Determinants of Homelessness and the Targeting of Housing Assistance," Journal of Urban Economics 55, 195–214.

Erber, E. (1977), "Impact of New Housing Construction on Racial Patterns," Journal Real Estate Economics 5, 313–336.

Fraumeni B. (1997), "The Measurement of Depreciation in the US National Income and Product Accounts," Survey of Current Business 2, 7–23.

Fulton, W. (1996), "The New Urbanism: Hope or Hype for American Communities?" Lincoln Institute of Land Policy: Cambridge, MA.

Garner, A. C. (2015), "Is Commercial Real Estate Reliving the 1980's and Early 1990's?" Federal Reserve Bank of Kansas City, Working Paper.

George, H. (1879), "Progress and Poverty: An Inquiry into the Cause of Industrial Depressions and of Increase of Want with Increase of Wealth; The Remedy," The Modern Library: New York.

Green, R. K. (2007), "Airports and Economic Development," Real Estate Economics 35, 91–112.

Gyouko, J. and A. Saiz (2004), "Reinvestment in the Housing Stock: The Role of Construction Costs and the Supply Side," Journal of Urban Economics 55, 238–256.

Hausman, J., B. H. Hall and Z. Griliches (1984), "Econometric Models for Count Data with an Application to the Patents – R & D Relationship," Econometrica 52, 909–938.

Lapping, M., R. Bevins and P. Herbers (1977), "Differential Assessment and Other Techniques to Preserve Missouri's Farmlands," Missouri Law Review 42, 369–408.

Ling, D. C. and W. R. Archer (2013), "Real Estate Principles: A Value Approach," 4th ed. US: McGraw-Hill Education, 625–628.

Lovell, S. and D. Sunding (2001), "Voluntary Development Restrictions and the Cost of Habitat Conservation," Real Estate Economics 29, 191–206.

Lyytikäinen, T. (2009), "Three-Rate Property Taxation and Housing Construction," Journal of Urban Economics 65, 305–313.

Luque, J. (2015), Urban Land Economics, Switzerland: Springer.

Luque, J. (2014), "Wages, Local Amenities, and the Rise of the Multi-skilled City," Annals of Regional Science 52, 457–467.

Luque, J. (2013), "Heterogeneous Tiebout Communities with Private Production and Anonymous Crowding," Regional Science and Urban Economics 43, 117–123.

Mayer, C. J. and C. T. Somerville (2000), "Residential Construction: Using the Urban Growth Model to Estimate Housing Supply," Journal of Urban Economics 48, 85–109.

McGrath, D (1996), "Urban Industrial Land Redevelopment and Contamination Risk," Journal of Urban Land Economics 47, 414–442.

Mian, A. and A. Sufi (2014), "House of Debt," The University of Chicago Press: Chicago, USA.

Munneke, H. J. (1996), "Redevelopment Decisions for Commercial and Industrial Properties," Journal of Urban Economics 39, 229–253.

Mutikani, L. (2015), "U.S. Housing Starts Approach Eight-Year High in July", US:Reuters. Thomson Reuters.

Natural Heritage Institute (1998), "Optimizing Habitat Conservation Planning on Non-Federal Lands," Natural Heritage Institute: San Francisco, CA.

Noonan, F. and C. A. Vidich (1992), "Decision Analysis for Utilizing Hazardous Waste Site Assessments in Real Estate Acquisition," Risk Analysis 12,
245–251.

Novy-Marx, R. (2005), "An Equilibrium Model of Investment Under Uncertainty," Working Paper. University of Chicago: Chicago, USA.

Plassman, F. and T. N. Tideman (2010), "A Markov Chain Monte Carlo Analysis
of the Effect of Two-Rate Property Taxes on Construction," Journal of Urban
Economics 47, 216–247.

Rosenthal, S. S. and R. W. Helsley (1994), "Redevelopment and the Urban Land
Price Gradient," Journal of Urban Economics 35, 182–200.

Saks, E. R. (2008), "Job Creation and Housing Construction: Constraints on
Metropolitan Area Employment Growth," Journal of Urban Economics 64,
178–195.

Sivitanidou, R. and P. Sivitanides (2000), "Does the Theory of Irreversible Investments Help Explain Movements in Office–Commercial Construction?" Real
Estate Economics 28, 623–661.

Solomon, A. (1977) "A National Policy and Budgetary Framework for Housing
and Community Development," AREUEA Journal 5, 147–170.

Sorensen, A., K. Taeuber and L. J. Hollingsworth (1974), "Indexes of Racial
Residential Segregation for 109 cities in the United States, 1940 to 1970,"
Institute for Research on Poverty, University of Wisconsin: Madison.

Topel, R. and S. Rosen (1988), "Housing Investment in the United States," Journal of Political Economy 96, 718–740.

Tu, C. and M. Eppli (2001), "An Empirical Examination of Traditional Neighborhood Development," Real Estate Economics 29, 485–501.

Turnbull, G. K. (1988), "Property Taxes and the Transition of Land to Urban
Use," The Journal of Real Estate Finance and Economics 1, 393–403.

Wheaton, W. C. (1982), "Urban Spatial Development with Durable but Replaceable Capital," Journal of Urban Economics 12, 53–67.

Index

OTHER TITLES IN OUR FINANCE AND FINANCIAL MANAGEMENT COLLECTION

John A. Doukas, Old Dominion University, *Editor*

- *Capital Budgeting* by Sandeep Goel
- *Online Marketing to Investors: How to Develop Effective Investor Relations* by Daniel R. Valentine
- *Essentials of Retirement Planning: A Holistic Review of Personal Retirement Planning Issues and Employer-Sponsored Plans, Third Edition* by Eric J. Robbins
- *Redefining Shareholder Value: Demystifying the Valuation Myth* by Mariana Schmid and Milan Frankl
- *Financial Ratios* by Sandeep Goel
- *Financial Services Sales Handbook: A Professionals Guide to Becoming a Top Producer* by Clifton T. Warren
- *Money Laundering and Terrorist Financing Activities: A Primer on Avoidance Management for Money Managers* by Milan Frankl and Ayse Ebru Kurcer

Announcing the Business Expert Press Digital Library

Concise e-books business students need for classroom and research

This book can also be purchased in an e-book collection by your library as

- *a one-time purchase,*
- *that is owned forever,*
- *allows for simultaneous readers,*
- *has no restrictions on printing, and*
- *can be downloaded as PDFs from within the library community.*

Our digital library collections are a great solution to beat the rising cost of textbooks. E-books can be loaded into their course management systems or onto student's e-book readers.

The **Business Expert Press** digital libraries are very affordable, with no obligation to buy in future years. For more information, please visit **www.businessexpertpress.com/librarians**. To set up a trial in the United States, please contact **sales@businessexpertpress.com**.

www.ingramcontent.com/pod-product-compliance
Lightning Source LLC
Chambersburg PA
CBHW050106210326
41519CB00015BA/3850